Black Belt
Krav Maga

Black Belt Krav Maga

Elite Techniques of the World's Most Powerful Combat System

DARREN LEVINE
RYAN HOOVER

Photographs by Dominic DiSaia

Ulysses Press

In memory of Marni Levine

Published in the United States by
ULYSSES PRESS
P.O. Box 3440
Berkeley, CA 94703
www.ulyssespress.com

Portions of the Use of Force (UOF) sections were drawn from the *California Jury Instructions—Criminal* (Fall 2008 edition), *California Peace Officer's Journal—Report Writing Guidelines* by D. Levine/M. Tavera and *UOF Commonly Asked Questions* (PowerPoint presentation for Krav Maga Worldwide) by E. Sheley/D. Levine.

ISBN: 978-1-56975-667-6
Library of Congress Control Number 2008911705

Printed in Canada by Webcom

10 9 8 7 6 5 4 3 2 1

Contributing writers	Kevin Lewis, Jarrett Arthur, Kor Morton
Acquisitions	Nick Denton-Brown
Editorial/Production	Lily Chou, Claire Chun, Lauren Harrison, Abigail Reser
Index	Sayre Van Young
Design	what!design @ whatweb.com
Photographs	Dominic DiSaia
Models	Jarrett Arthur, Otis Berry, Kelly Campbell, Pawel Cichowlas, Jeff Frederickson, Ryan Hoover, Darren Levine, Kevin Lewis, Kor Morton, Eric Powell, Sam Sade, Dan Sovetky, Chris Torres

Visit Krav Maga Worldwide online at www.kravmaga.com

Distributed by Publishers Group West

Please Note

This book has been written and published strictly for informational purposes, and in no way should be used as a substitute for actual instruction with qualified professionals. The author and publisher are providing you with information in this work so that you can have the knowledge and can choose, at your own risk, to act on that knowledge. The author and publisher also urge all readers to be aware of their health status and to consult health care professionals before beginning any health program.

Table of Contents

About This Book

Black Belt Krav Maga is a compilation of advanced techniques selected from Krav Maga Worldwide's carefully designed and vastly evolved Black Belt Level curriculum. Like *Krav Maga for Beginners* and *Complete Krav Maga*, this book is not meant to be a complete and exhaustive description of all Krav Maga black belt techniques; rather, it features unique training modules selected from some of our system's most advanced hand-to-hand combat and defensive tactics material.

This book will address sophisticated handgun threats, carjacking scenarios, our approach to third-party protection, edged-weapon threats, defending edged-weapon attacks by using a blunt object or edged weapon, defending blunt objects with blunt objects, and performing progressive tactics and techniques to neutralize hand grenade and improvised explosive device (I.E.D.) threats. Needless to say, all of the topics presented are extremely high risk and involve the potential use of deadly force. Some of the sections will be based more on principle than technique, taking into account the many variables that may affect intricate technical responses.

This book also provides some general information about the actual weapons, the assailants and, where applicable, weapons to be used for defensive and/or offensive functions. It also discusses training methodologies, use of force, legal considerations and more.

It's important to note that this book was not written in an effort to replace training with an updated and presently certified Krav Maga Worldwide instructor. This book is meant to serve as a resource for advanced instructors and an introduction for other instructors and students wishing to further their knowledge in the system. It bears repeating that the scenarios presented in this book are of extreme high risk, and no medium can replace actual supervised training.

What Is Krav Maga?

Krav Maga was originally developed in Israel as the official system of self-defense and hand-to-hand combat for the Israeli Defense Forces, the Israeli National Police, Israeli Special Operations and other security units. More recently, Krav Maga has been taught extensively to civilians, law-enforcement agencies and military units in the United States, and to our allies throughout the world. Cognizant of the different use-of-force standards between Israel and the United States, important steps were taken by Krav Maga Worldwide to refine and adapt Krav Maga techniques for use by American law enforcement and civilians.

More information about the history of Krav Maga can be found in *Complete Krav Maga* and *Krav Maga for Beginners*.

The System

Krav Maga emerged in an environment where extreme violence was common. Krav Maga has a worldwide reputation as being an ideal means of defending one's life, or the life of a third party, whether the threat involves unarmed assailants, armed assailants or multiple assailants. The Krav Maga Worldwide system has received international recognition as an innovative and highly practical self-defense system ideally suited for three distinct entities: law enforcement, military and civilians.

Potentially lethal-force scenarios in this book include: advanced threats involving a handgun, carjacking scenarios involving handgun threats within and around motor vehicles, handgun defenses when the attack is directed at a third party, defenses against threats with an edged weapon, using a blunt weapon or common object to defend against a blunt weapon attack, using a blunt weapon, edged weapon or common object to defend against an edged weapon, and threats involving an assailant with an explosive device.

Perhaps the most important characteristics of the system are:

Practical Techniques   The main emphasis of the Krav Maga system is on effectiveness, simplicity and sound, logical problem solving. This is a street-fighting system that provides realistic defenses against a variety of aggressive attacks, whether the assailant is armed or unarmed, and whether the attack is directed at you or a third party. The system is well integrated, which means techniques and principles that are taught will be applicable in more than one situation, allowing students to learn to deal with reaction time, defenses and counterattacks that will apply to a multitude of different attacks.

Efficient Training Period   Students attain a high level of proficiency in a relatively short period of instruction. Krav Maga training today has been further refined to meet the needs of citizens and law-enforcement personnel tasked with other priorities, missions, endeavors and responsibilities in daily life. Krav Maga Worldwide's training methodology is specifically designed to build a warrior in a minimal amount of time, and the system allows students to achieve life-saving skills in a relatively short period of time.

Retention of Training   The Krav Maga system is based on common principles and natural, instinctive reactions to danger. It's due to these facts that Krav Maga techniques can be retained with minimal review and practice.

Darren Levine (right) demonstrates the appropriate way to defend against a stick attack.

Performing Techniques Under Stress and Other Conditions That Replicate Reality Unique training methods are a key ingredient to the Krav Maga system and are specifically designed to replicate the realities that exist in a true life-threatening encounter. The training is designed to improve one's emotional and physical response to danger. Unique training methods are used to develop the ability to recognize danger at its earliest stages, to go from a non- or low state of readiness to a state of action without hesitation, to develop a warrior's mindset, to engage and overcome an adversary, and to escalate and to deescalate to appropriate levels of force.

Use of Force Issues Krav Maga Worldwide training enables people to defend themselves and deal with the most violent armed assailants they encounter, while remaining acutely aware of reasonable use of force and civil liabilities that arise during a violent encounter.

Training Methodology

While many of Krav Maga's techniques and tactics are certainly singular in their effectiveness, it is the exclusive delivery system that Krav Maga Worldwide utilizes to train its operators that quite possibly sets it apart from other self-defense training systems. Techniques, in a vacuum, are useless. Without developing aggressiveness or fighting spirit in students, the techniques will not matter, because under duress the defender will be unable to react in a timely or effective manner. The student/defender must train in a way that will promote and enhance decisive action under extreme stress and/or fatigue. Therefore, Krav Maga Worldwide places a great premium on "training methodology" as one of the most important ways to enhance survivability in a violent encounter. An up-to-date, certified Krav Maga Worldwide instructor is not only tasked with teaching techniques in a manner that can be assimilated quickly, but devising and implementing training methods and drills that allow students to gain confidence and pressure-test abilities (in a relatively safe environment).

In Krav Maga training sessions, the emphasis is on "replicating reality." By studying real-life violent encounters, we discover where victims fall prey to aggressors. What is it that occurs during a fight for one's life where people fail in their effort to react correctly to specific and non-specific dangers directed at them? The use of creative training methods to build the desired physiological and emotional response to danger is as vital as the physical techniques that exist in a defensive tactics system. What happens when an assailant really wants to hurt, torture, rape and/or kill you? Has your training included operating under the stress of real-life conditions?

Students should be trained in a way that pushes limits, overwhelming them physically and emotionally. One must be forced to fight when attention is seriously challenged and divided, when vision is impaired and when fatigue of the body tries to persuade the mind and spirit to quit. Pushing students to these limits conditions them to control breathing, auditory and visual impairments and the like while in a combative situation—to keep fighting even if shot, stabbed or broken.

This section is not meant to be a tutorial on how to structure a Krav Maga class, nor will it address all of the training methods incorporated into Krav Maga Worldwide classes. The purpose of this section is to introduce and detail elements of training that should be a part of any good self-defense system.

Position of Disadvantage
As addressed in previous books, Krav Maga self-defense techniques are almost always trained from a neutral position or from a position of disadvantage. While it's certainly possible that a defender recognizes a threat early, training from a position of disadvantage (in the dark, with the emergence of an unknown threat or threats, while physically exhausted, with divided attention, having to make multiple tactical decisions in a correct sequence, functioning while injured or from a restricted position, etc.) is designed to inculcate in one a warrior spirit and skill sets that help one to overcome physical, emotional and spiritual obstacles. In other words, since students are often put into worst-case situations in their training sessions, performing in a true-life encounter where one is required to defend when more distracted, with a lower state of readiness, fear, etc., permits them to succeed because the training methods employed help them to react and perform effectively under the conditions they will face in real combat. They succeed because "you perform as you train" (or maybe even less) and the training drills have specifically prepared them to succeed under such dire circumstances.

Unfamiliar Surroundings
In addition to training from positions of disadvantage (in reference to the student's body), it's also important to train in unfamiliar and less-controlled surroundings. Always training on matted floors, with mirrors and familiar points of reference, is not conducive to the most realistic training. Therefore, students should be exposed to training in areas such as parks, offices, parking garages/lots, vehicles, etc. The unfamiliar surroundings, in addition to varying terrains and obstacles, will broaden a student's understanding of the need for different solutions under different conditions. It's also fun!

Scenario Replication
Scenario replication is a vital part of Krav Maga Worldwide training. Simply changing environments or body postures, without situational scenarios, is not enough. In order for students to learn to critically analyze danger in an environment and gain situational awareness, they must apply Krav Maga principles appropriately. They should be put to the test by using creative and relevant facts to enhance the training session. Situational drills will often determine appropriate pre-contact behavior, defensive techniques, tactics, use of force, etc. For example, a 35-year-old man "placed" in an elevator with one seemingly inebriated and slightly agitated 60-year-old man would likely undergo completely different adrenal, technical and tactical responses than the same man carrying his 10-month-old baby on an elevator with three belligerent and argumentative 20-year-olds. Without creative scenarios based on accurate accounts of real street crime, it's difficult for students to imagine circumstances that would force different physiological and tactical responses. Moreover, it's extremely difficult to react decisively under varying circumstances if training only consists of compliant or relatively compliant partners, in which the context is always the same or is never addressed.

Training Partners
It's massively important to train with others and to train with as many different types of people as you can: short, tall, young, old, big, small, athletic, fast, strong, etc. A resisting "opponent" is invaluable to realistic self-defense training, and everyone has a different "feel," a different energy and a different approach. Being exposed to these differences is important to practical training.

Training Drills

Finally, training drills bring all of the other components together. Drills in Krav Maga classes account for anywhere from 10 to 30 percent of the allotted time, but training drills comprise as much as 50 percent of the total system. This is important to note since some other systems have great techniques and poor training drills, while others have poor techniques but great training drills. The Krav Maga Worldwide approach is to give equal or nearly equal relevance and attention to both.

How do professional football players prepare for game day? You may be surprised to learn that very little of practice time is devoted to actually playing inter-squad games. Training consists of the use of thoughtful, creative and carefully devised training drills that, in a concentrated format, improve skill sets and mentally prepares player for the stress of high-level, violent competition. Therefore, the effective use of drills must replicate the conditions present in a professional football game. In reality, the training session should bring the athlete to a point where performing in the game is easier than the high-level drills they must perform in preparation for a contest. Players must be pushed to their limits physically, emotionally, spiritually in practice sessions, without being injured, so that they're available at game time. These practice sessions should produce the same chemical, physiological and psychological responses that exist during an official and highly contested war-like game.

In dealing with deadly force scenarios, it's obvious that we cannot train under 100 percent realistic conditions. If we did, we would severely, even fatally, injure participants during the training sessions. So, how can we prepare our students to survive violence, not only the physical attack but also the assault that is inflicted on all their senses and emotions? Trainers must build the mind-body component that ultimately controls whether or not one can respond with an effective physical technique to defeat an aggressor. You may be able to kick and punch in a controlled environment, but how do you respond when you're in tremendous fear, when you're fatigued, when your attention is divided, when you're injured but you must keep fighting? What good is it to learn effective techniques inside a controlled training room? It means nothing if you're not able to manage your body and mind and perform the defensive principles and techniques you've learned over hours, weeks, months and years of training.

Every training drill must have at least a singular purpose to prepare the student for that which he/she will need in a street war. Every training drill must challenge the defender to perform under the most uncomfortable conditions, in which each one of their senses and emotions is tapped, tested and severely challenged. Stress inoculation is a way to train people in preparation for battle. Students can be trained to avoid freezing during a violent encounter. Students can be trained to see when tunnel vision is occurring. Students can learn to "manage" physiological and emotional responses in order to operate at maximum capacity, while maintaining situational awareness. Students can be trained to control breathing in order to reduce fatigue. Students can be taught to overcome fear and turn fear into a positive force for survival.

While there are many benefits to training drills, some of the most important are:

- Improved reaction time
- Improved vision and awareness of the environment
- Controlling fatigue by breathing while under stress
- Ability to make correct tactical decisions while functioning under stress
- Enhanced critical thinking and physical performance
- Overcoming fear and confusion when being hit or disturbed
- Increased student confidence
- Better understanding of techniques, principles and goals
- Improved class morale
- Improved fitness level using a combat-functional process
- Increased class energy

There are many genres of drills that can be employed to achieve these goals. For the purposes of this book, we'll highlight four:

Aggressiveness Drills: Designed to develop or enhance fighting spirit in students; such drills often require students to get through some sort of barrier or obstacle before, after or while performing combatives or self-defense.

Fatigue Drills: Designed to push students to and just beyond a feeling of exhaustion and motivate them to do even more; fatigue drills typically involve a lot of aerobic and/or anaerobic movements devised to exhaust specific body parts or the entire body.

Awareness Drills: Designed to increase students' ability to recognize and/or track current threats or impending threats; these drills often require students to identify a target or threat and respond with the appropriate combative or tactical reaction, often while performing other tasks.

Stress Drills: Designed to develop or enhance the ability to perform under varying levels or types of stress; such drills typically require students to perform more than one task at a time, switch from one activity to another quickly, respond under extreme duress and/or uncomfortable circumstances, and may combine elements of other drill types .

Below you'll find a sample of Krav Maga training methods to create effective and correct responses for real-life, horrific and violent encounters. Krav Maga Worldwide instructors have been exposed to hundreds of similar drills, and all of the drills listed here can be modified for basic or advanced students. The training methodologies employed by Krav Maga Worldwide are intended to get students to a level of proficiency quickly, while providing a realistic yet safe and enjoyable training experience.

When designing or implementing drills, it's vital to understand the goal of the drill and any inherent dangers. It's also important to make sure that principles are not violated as a result of the design of the drill. For example, do not create a drill that trades sound tactics for aggressiveness. Drills are essential to real Krav Maga training, but poorly designed or implemented drills can be dangerous and counterproductive to students. Ultimately, the more variables students can be exposed to in training without severely compromising their safety, the better prepared they will be should they ever find themselves facing a violent encounter.

1. Down–Up Drill

PEOPLE NEEDED 2

SKILLS NEEDED Stance, straight punches

EQUIPMENT 1 tombstone pad

DRILL The student punches the tombstone pad at 50–60 percent speed/power. When the instructor yells "Down!" the student sprawls into a push-up position, springs to his feet, and proceeds to punch the pad at 100 percent speed/power until the instructor yells "Time!" The student returns to 50–60 percent speed afterward and waits for the next command.

VARIATIONS

1. Target is stationary in the original exercise. To make it more difficult, the pad holder sprints to a new location in the room while the partner is sprawling.

2. When the instructor calls "Down!" he also calls a direction left or right. The student performs a log roll in that direction until the instructor calls "time!" The student then gets up.

SAFETY IN TRAINING

• Make sure all punchers are facing the same direction. Do not combine variations 1 and 2.

• Explain how pads should be held.

2. Find Your Partner Drill

PEOPLE NEEDED 2

SKILLS NEEDED Stance, straight punches

EQUIPMENT 1 tombstone pad

DRILL Partner A lies face down with eyes closed. Partner B moves to a spot in the room. The instructor yells "Go!" Partner A gets up quickly, surveys the room for Partner B, sprints to him, and then attacks with straight punches.

VARIATIONS

1. Vary the combatives.
2. Turn off the lights.
3. Add obstacles to the room.

SAFETY IN TRAINING

- Remind students to be careful not to collide.
- Explain how pads should be held.

3. Combatives with Strength Exercise Drill

PEOPLE NEEDED 2

SKILLS NEEDED Stance, straight punches

EQUIPMENT 1 tombstone pad or kick shield

DRILL Partner A holds the tombstone pad with his back to a wall. Partner B punches the pad at 60 percent speed/power. When the instructor yells "Go!" Partner B sprints to the opposite end of the room and drops and does 5 or 10 push-ups. Partner B then sprints back and attacks the tombstone at 100 percent speed/power. When the instructor yells "Time!" Partner B returns to punching at 60 percent speed/power.

VARIATIONS

1. Turn off the lights.

2. Have students give knees instead.

3. Have students do squats rather than push-ups.

- Remind students to have control when re-engaging target after sprinting.
- Explain how pads should be held.

4. Touch the Knee Drill

PEOPLE NEEDED 2

SKILLS NEEDED stance and movement

EQUIPMENT None

DRILL Students face one another in fighting stance about 5 or 6 feet away from one another. One is the attacker and the other the defender. The attacker lunges forward, attempting to touch the defender's knee. The defender, while maintaining a good fighting stance, tries to evade the attack by moving his feet.

Notes: The attacker must attack EACH TIME from a distance of 5 or 6 feet. The defender should make it a point to move his feet and not fall into to the trap of keeping his feet still while moving his hips back. Level changes should be made by bending at the knees, not at the waist.

VARIATIONS

1. The attacker touches the shoulder.
2. The defender can use his hand to block the attack

SAFETY IN TRAINING

- Warn students to beware of head butts.

5. Double-Hand Balance Drill

PEOPLE NEEDED 2

SKILLS NEEDED None

EQUIPMENT None

DRILL Students stand facing one another approximately 1 ½ feet apart; feet are shoulder width and hands are raised to approximately shoulder level. With palms facing one another, each student simultaneously tries to draw the other off balance. This is done by briskly pushing or pulling the opponent's hands only. Students should be loose and allow their hands to absorb any changes in balance.

6. Combatives Crossing Drill

PEOPLE NEEDED 4

SKILLS NEEDED Punches/Knees

EQUIPMENT 1 tombstone pad, 1 kick shield

DRILL Two pairs of partners (at least) line up on opposite sides of the room. One pair has a tombstone pad and a puncher, while the other has a kick shield and a student prepared to give knees. When the drill begins, students attack the pads with the appropriate weapon. When the instructor yells "Switch!" students giving combatives run across the room and begin attacking the new target (if the student was punching, he now knees, and vice versa). When the instructor yells "Switch!" again, they return to their original partner. This repeats until the instructor calls "Time!" at which time the group switches roles.

Note: This drill works best when students have to crisscross each other while running across the room. For example, some groups should run north–south, others run east–west and others run on a diagonal in between.

VARIATIONS

1. If your class is divisible by 3, add 1 student in the middle (place the third student between the other two and this student runs back and forth giving combatives while the other two hold pads).

2. Just punch or just give knees—don't mix combatives.

SAFETY IN TRAINING

- This drill can be somewhat dangerous because the students can very easily run into each other. Before beginning the drill, the instructor must tell the students: "NO ONE GETS HURT IN THIS DRILL! YOU GET TO THE OTHER SIDE OF THE ROOM AS FAST AS YOU POSSIBLY CAN WITHOUT AS MUCH AS BRUSHING AGAINST ANYONE'S SHOULDER."

- Explain how pads should be held.

7. Pad Scramble

PEOPLE NEEDED Minimum of 8

SKILLS NEEDED Straight punches or knees

EQUIPMENT Punch shields or kick shields

DRILL Divide the class into 2 groups and line the groups on opposite sides of the room. Place one pad for every 2 students in the center of the room (for example, if there are 20 students, place 10 pads in the center of the room). Students start lying face down, facing away from the pads. On the instructor's command, students crawl as fast as possible toward the pile of pads. Students who get to the pads first get to hold, while the others have to punch the pads for 30 seconds. Repeat 3 to 5 times.

- Students must CRAWL, not run, to the pads, to minimize dangers.
- Explain how pads should be held.

8. Breaking through the Crowd Drill

PEOPLE NEEDED 6 to 10 per group

SKILLS NEEDED Varies

EQUIPMENT Varies

DRILL This drill is a variation on many distraction drills used to create situations in which the defender does not know where or when the attack will come. The defender stands a few feet away from a crowd of people with his eyes closed. While the defender's eyes are closed, the instructor silently designates one person in the crowd to be the attacker. On the instructor's command, the defender opens his eyes and walks through the middle of the crowd, which is also walking toward him. If and when he is attacked, he responds aggressively.

Notes: The type of attack should be appropriate to the class level. For beginning students, the attack should be the one worked on in that class. For beginners with more experience, the attack should be one of several (attacker's choice). As students become more advanced, add weapon attacks/threats to this same drill.

VARIATIONS

1. In some instances, no attacker should be assigned to keep the defender from maintaining a high state of readiness.

2. If the group is large enough, more than one attacker could be assigned.

3. Attackers should sometimes be at the front of the crowd, sometimes in the middle and sometimes in the back.

9. Disturbing Combinations on Focus Mitts Drill

PEOPLE NEEDED 2

SKILLS NEEDED Straight punches

EQUIPMENT Focus mitts

DRILL The focus mitt holder attacks his partner while wearing mitts. The holder will punch, kick, knee and generally disturb the puncher. The holder should be aggressive. When the holder claps, he separates from his partner. The puncher will throw an immediate left/right combination. When not active, the puncher should do his best to cover and absorb.

VARIATIONS

1. Instructor can limit attacks (e.g., punches only) that the holder has at his disposal.
2. Instructor can change the combination the puncher throws.

SAFETY IN TRAINING

- The holder must clap mitts when separating. The audible cue insures both partners know what comes next.
- Explain how mitts should be held.

10. Interference Drills

PEOPLE NEEDED 3 or 4

SKILLS NEEDED Basic combatives (punches will do)

EQUIPMENT Kick shield and protective equipment (headgear for the disturbers and attackers)

DRILL One person holds the pad while the other attacks it fiercely with combatives. The third person tries to keep the attacker off of the bag by pushing, pulling, standing in between, etc., using the kick shield as interference. The attacker must get beyond the disturber and attack the bag; however, the attacker cannot attack the disturber. The attacker can pull the disturber out of the way or push him, but he cannot punch or kick him. The attacker's main goal is to attack the bag ferociously.

VARIATIONS

1. Add an additional disturber.

2. If there's only a group of 2, the attacker can attack a heavy bag. If there's one extra person, that person should be put in a group of 3, giving the group one extra disturber.

SAFETY IN TRAINING

- The person most likely to get hurt is the disturber. Warn the students of this. Ideally, the disturber wears headgear and a mouthpiece.
- Explain how pads should be held.

11. Plow the Field Drill

PEOPLE NEEDED 3

SKILLS NEEDED Straight punches, hammerfists, palm heel strikes

EQUIPMENT 1 tombstone pad, 1 belt (long)

DRILL The puncher stands in a fighting stance with a belt around his waist, ready to attack the tombstone pad. One partner stands in front of the puncher holding the pad, while the other stands behind the puncher holding on to the belt. When the instructor says "Go!" the puncher attacks the pad with straight punches, hammerfists, and palm heel strikes. The partner holding the belt pulls to keep the puncher away from the pad; the belt holder should make it difficult, but not impossible, for the puncher to succeed. The instructor should let the puncher train for approximately 1 minute.

VARIATIONS

1. The third partner can be replaced by a heavy bag.

2. If the student knows the forward hard fall break, the partner holding the belt can periodically drop the belt around the puncher's ankles and pull his feet from underneath him.

SAFETY IN TRAINING

- The belt holder cannot suddenly let go of the belt.
- Explain how pads should be held.

12. Roaming Attackers Drill

PEOPLE NEEDED 12 minimum

SKILLS NEEDED At least 1 self-defense technique, but works best with several different techniques

EQUIPMENT None

DRILL Divide the class into groups of As and Bs. The As close their eyes while the Bs roam through the room and attack the As with some sort of grab (choke, headlock, bearhug, or any or all of them). The As defend and counter, then close their eyes to wait for the next attack.

VARIATIONS

1. For beginning students, defenses should be done relatively slowly. With more-advanced students, feel free to add stress to the drill. For example:
   a. Turn off the lights.
   b. Play loud music.
   c. The instructor can roam the room and disturb the defenders by pushing them, shoving them, spinning them, etc.
   d. Use big exercise balls and throw them at the defenders while they wait for the attack.

- Warn the students to maintain control. This drill can be scary and stressful. Often, when students are scared, they lose control and technique goes out the window.
- Explain how pads should be held.

13. All Class A/B Drill

PEOPLE NEEDED 2

SKILLS NEEDED Knees

EQUIPMENT 1 kick shield

DRILL At the beginning of class, each pair of students will select an "A" and a "B." These will be the designated positions for the remainder of the class. At any time during class, the instructor will yell either "A" or "B." If the instructor yells "A," the student with the "A" designation will abandon the current task and sprint to pick up a kick shield. The student with the "B" designation finds "A" and gives knees repeatedly until the instructor calls "Time!" The drill should be done at awkward moments when the students least expect it (during lectures, breaks, in the middle of another exercise, during instruction, etc.).

VARIATIONS

1. Combatives can be changed.

SAFETY IN TRAINING

- Students should be careful when running to the pad.
- Explain how pads should be held.

14. A, B and Both Defending Punches or Kicks Drill

PEOPLE NEEDED 2

SKILLS NEEDED Any punch or kick defenses

EQUIPMENT Only the equipment one would need for the particular defenses. For example, shin guards would be a good idea when working on kick defenses.

DRILL Students work in pairs with one as an "A" and one as a "B." The letter the instructor calls is the attacker, and the other is the defender. For example, when the instructor calls "A," "A" attacks and "B" defends. When the instructor calls "Both," both students attack AND defend. The instructor goes from "A" to "B" to both somewhat randomly; however, it's important to keep the "both" portion short in the beginning.

1. This can be done with any punch defense or kick defense or multiple defenses.

SAFETY IN TRAINING

• Be sure all students have proper training gear and the basic knowledge needed for this drill.

15. Flank Attack Drill

PEOPLE NEEDED 3

EQUIPMENT 2 kick shields

DRILL Two people hold pads. One stands in front of the defender, who works basic punches and elbows at the pad. The second person comes up from behind and gives a verbal signal. On the signal, the defender sends a back kick, then turns and delivers a few punches as knees. AS EARLY AS POSSIBLE, the defender should also "spin" the second pad holder so that he is a shield between the defender and the first pad holder. Once the defender has done this, he should begin basic work on this second pad. The first pad holder moves around, delivers a verbal threat from behind, and the drill continues. Have students go for 1 to 2 minutes before switching. It's exhausting but great!

VARIATIONS

1. Vary combatives.
2. Introduce another partner as an attacker or disturber.

SAFETY IN TRAINING

• Be sure the student holding for the back kick is close enough for the defender to reach.
• Explain how pads should be held.

Use of Force:
The Rules of Self-Defense

If you are reading this book, it is safe to assume that you have an interest in developing your ability to defend yourself. If you are physically attacked as a target of an aggravated assault, a rape, an attempted murder or some other violent crime, having the physical and tactical skills to survive the encounter may truly be a matter of life and death.

Self-defense instructors often teach their students to win at all costs—to do anything and everything to survive, to punish the assailant for assaulting you. Some may believe these statements to be true; however, such advice is usually proclaimed out of context and may have significant, negative, long-term, life-changing ramifications that involve legal battles in both civil and criminal arenas. You should be familiar with use of force law and its effect on your right to use self-defense, even deadly force, should the need arise. The saying "It's better to be judged by a jury of 12 than carried by a group of six" is a truism and is also a gross oversimplification of the law. You must be prepared to win the battle on the street, while conducting yourself lawfully and ethically so that you survive the legal battles that may follow in the courts.

The area of law commonly referred to as "use of force" has applications in both civil and criminal contexts. Established principles give civilians the right to apply force to the person of another, to engage in violence for the sole purpose of defending one's own life or the life of a third party from physical harm, great bodily injury, and/or even death.

"Force" is defined as any physical effort to defend against an assault or battery, or any physical action designed to control and restrain another, or force used to overcome resistance from another person. Generally, people may lawfully react in self-defense, and are authorized to do so, only if they use an amount of force that is reasonable to maintain their personal safety.

The standard of review is an objective one. "Objectively reasonable" means that the defender shall evaluate each situation requiring the use of force in light of the known circumstances (including, but not limited to, the seriousness of the attack or crime being directed at them, the level of threat or resistance presented by the attacker, the danger to others present at the scene, or the danger to the community) in determining the necessity for force and the appropriate level of force.

What Is the "Reasonable Person" Standard?

The phrase "reasonable person" is frequently used in both civil and criminal law to describe a hypothetical or fictional person in the community who exercises average care, skill and judgment in conduct and who serves as a comparative standard for determining liability. The decision whether an accused person is guilty or civilly liable of a given offense, or liable in a civil action, may well involve the application of an objective test in which the conduct of the accused is compared to that of a reasonable person under the same or similar circumstances. In most cases, persons with greater than average skills, or with special duties to society, are held to a higher standard of care.

Once the danger has been eliminated and the assailant is controlled, the defender must stop applying force and inflicting injury; otherwise, his actions may no longer qualify as "self-defense" but take on the element of delivering punishment to the original attacker. Such action is likely to be considered an "unreasonable" application of force.

Legal Implications Relating to the Doctrine of Self-Defense

The doctrine of self-defense may vary from one jurisdiction to another. Generally, the act of self-defense or the defense of another may serve to excuse, justify or mitigate one from criminal and/or civil liability. For example, if you apply force against another person, you may face misdemeanor or felony criminal charges as a direct result of your actions. If the criminal charges are proved beyond a reasonable doubt, you could face jail time, confinement in state prison, fines and restitution to be paid to the injured party.

A separate and distinct form of liability may subject you to a civil lawsuit. If you inflict physical injuries and/or emotional harm to another by acting outside the scope of your right to self-defense, but your actions do not rise to the level of criminal conduct, you may be responsible for payment of monetary compensation and be subject to additional court-imposed orders. Generally, in a civil suit the victim seeks money and in a criminal case the government seeks punishment for a crime.

A clear distinction in self-defense is to eliminate force that is being unlawfully directed at you by responding appropriately with a reasonable level of force to protect yourself from imminent harm. You must use a level of violence that is reasonable, comparable or proportionate to the threat faced. For example, you may only use deadly force for defensive purposes in situations of "extreme" danger. The claim of a right to self-defense would fail, for example, if someone asserted the right of self-defense, but used deadly force that resulted in the deliberate killing of a perpetrator of a minor crime, although the criminal did not appear to be a physical threat to anyone.

When Is Use of Force "Self-Defense"?

Technically speaking, it is lawful for a person who is being assaulted to defend against a physical attack, as long as a reasonable person has grounds for believing, and actually does believe, that bodily injury is about to be inflicted. If that is the case, that person may use all physical force that they believe to be reasonably necessary and which would appear to a reasonable person, in the same or similar circumstances, to be necessary to prevent the injury that appears to be imminent. In addition, it is lawful for a person who, as a reasonable person, has reason for believing and actually does believe that bodily injury is about to be inflicted upon another person to protect that individual from attack. In that situation, they may use all force that that person believes to be reasonably necessary and which would appear to a reasonable person, in the same or similar circumstances, to be necessary to prevent the injury that appears to be imminent.

In simpler terms, one such scenario in which self-defense may be legally justified is when a person is assaulted; the defender is not bound to retreat, even though a retreat might safely be made. Similarly, a person could also use reasonable force to defend another individual from injury or an attack. The same applies to the defense of private property. In the case of private dwellings, businesses or vehicles (according to the U.S. Castle Doctrine, and depending on the state), a person can resist an intruder's violent or unlawful entry with force, increasing it in proportion to the intruder's persistence and violence; as with personal self-defense, the defender is not bound to retreat, even though a retreat might safely be made.

If two individuals engage in mutual combat, the right of self-defense is only available if the defender has:

1. Actually attempted, in good faith, to refuse to continue fighting;

2. By words or conduct, caused the opponent to be aware, as a reasonable person, that he desires to stop fighting;

After-Actions Suggestions

- Contact the police and your legal counsel as soon as possible.

- If you or the assailant is injured, obtain medical treatment by notifying the proper authorities.

- If available, obtain witness statements. The use of audiotape is strongly recommended to preserve witness statements and to prevent a change in a witness's testimony at a later date.

- Obtain the names and address of all individuals present and document their observations or lack of observations.

- If you have pain or visible injury, use a 35mm or digital camera, whenever possible, to photograph the injured area. The photographs of the area should be before and after treatment by medical personnel. The post-medical treatment photograph should show the area without the bandage or covering, or if you have disheveled and torn clothing, this should also be photographed

- If the aggressor complains of pain or has visible injury, summon the required medical treatment and even apply first aid if safe and necessary to do so.

3. By words or conduct, caused the opponent to be aware, as a reasonable person, that he has in fact stopped fighting; and

4. Has given the opponent the opportunity to stop fighting.

After the defender has done these four things, he has the right to self-defense if the opponent continues to fight. In some countries and U.S. states, the notion of "pre-emptive" self-defense is limited by a condition that the threat be imminent. Thus, lawful "pre-emptive" self-defense is simply the act of landing the first blow in a situation that has reached a point for no de-escalation, resolution or escape. Many people believe that if the situation is so obvious as to feel assured that violence is inescapable, the defender has a much better probability of surviving by landing the first blow and gaining the immediate upper hand to quickly stop the risk to their person.

Actual Danger Not Necessary

"Actual danger" is not necessary as good reason for acting in self-defense. If a person is confronted by the outward show of danger of which they are mindful, and as a reasonable person, they possess an actual *belief and fear* that they are about to suffer bodily injury, the person's right of self-defense is the same whether the danger itself is authentic or only apparent. The right of self-defense, however, exists only as long as the real or apparent threatened danger continues to exist. When the danger ceases to appear to exist, the right to use force in self-defense ends. It's that simple.

Deadly Force

A person may exercise deadly force in self-defense or in the defense of others only when he reasonably believes that death or serious bodily injury is about to be inflicted upon himself or some other third party. In other words, the threat is *about to happen* and is not unclear as to when it may occur sometime in the future.

"Homicide" refers to the act of killing another human being. This is commonly referred to as death "at the hands of another." Homicide is not always an illegal act; criminal homicide arises when a person purposely, knowingly, recklessly or negligently causes the death of another. Homicide is considered to be justifiable and not unlawful when committed by any person who is defending an attempt by an assailant to commit a forcible and atrocious felony. Some commonly used examples of forcible and atrocious crimes are murder, mayhem, torture, kidnap, robbery or rape.

Whether defending oneself or the life of another, mere groundless fear of death or great bodily injury is not enough to justify a homicide. To justify taking the life of another person in self-defense, the danger must be apparent, present and immediate, and instantly dealt with, or must appear to be so at the time the defender uses deadly force. The killing must also be done under a well-founded, good faith, reasonable belief that it is necessary to save oneself from death or great bodily harm.

Golden Rules of Self-Defense and Commonly Asked Questions

GOLDEN RULE #1   You may use no greater force than a reasonable person would deem necessary to defend against the threat proffered.

Q: What constitutes a "threat" under this rule?
A: It varies significantly by state, but always includes physical harm against yourself or others; some states include crimes against property as well.

Q: I'm a martial arts expert. How does that affect what I can do?
A: If you *know* that your assailant is unskilled and unarmed, you can't respond with more force than necessary to eliminate the threat.

Q: What if I don't know the skill level of my assailant?
A: If a reasonable person would *think* that use of your martial arts abilities was necessary to eliminate the threat (generally the case with most situations involving thugs in dark alleys), it doesn't matter if that is true in *fact*.

Q: When can I use deadly force?
A: A person may not use deadly force unless he reasonably believes that:

a) The assailant is using or about to use deadly physical force or force likely to inflict great bodily injury.

or

b) Is about to commit any other crime specified by the state in question (usually burglary, arson rape or kidnapping; sometimes robbery and other forcible and atrocious crimes, but that varies).

GOLDEN RULE #2 Once the threat is eliminated, you cannot continue to use force.

Q: Does that mean if my assailant retreats I cannot continue to fight him?
A: Yes, unless he poses a threat to someone else.

Q: Does that mean if I myself can retreat to avoid the confrontation, I must do so?
A: Maybe, but not necessarily. Roughly half of the states have a "retreat rule" while the other half apply the "true man" doctrine.

Q: What happens if I'm fighting with someone I share my home with?
A: The law is unsettled in this area, but many states are considering an exception to the Castle Doctrine for cohabitants.

GOLDEN RULE #3 Don't be the aggressor.

Q: What if I only started a fist fight and the guy pulls a knife on me? Can't self-defense be a justification then?
A: Probably not. Most jurisdictions prevent even non-lethal aggressors from using self-defense as a justification if they later use lethal force to defend against lethal force. *Some* jurisdictions will allow this, however; again, know the law in your state.

Know the Law in Your State!

Retreat Rule:

If you *know* you can retreat without risking injury, you must do so.

"True Man" Doctrine:

If you did not initiate the encounter, you are not obligated to retreat (so long as your assailant still poses a threat) even if you can do so safely.

Castle Doctrine:

An exception to the retreat rule: If you are in your own home, you are not obligated to retreat, even under a state following the retreat rule.

Peterson Doctrine:

If you're the initial aggressor you can't use self-defense as a justification for a use of force, unless you've made a good-faith showing that you wanted to stop fighting.

Use of Force Reporting Guidelines

Civilians have generally not been trained to write reports that document the general nature of the events that took place during a Use of Force incident. However, current trends in civil litigation and allegations of excessive force suggest a need to reevaluate the philosophy. Therefore, it may be prudent for those who have been involved in a use of force incident to memorialize it in a truthful, detailed and comprehensive manner, as described below. You should write the reports in plain English and avoid whenever possible the use of legalese.

Recommended Procedures

Documentation should occur whenever there is a significant application of force to another. The use of force should be documented. You may also want to utilize a Use of Force Report Checklist, which should help to organize your thoughts and to memorialize the use of force incident in a detailed and accurate manner. A number of items can be addressed in the documentation, including but not limited to:

Defense of Third Parties

Old Rule:

The defender stands in the shoes of the person he's defending and if that person doesn't have a right IN FACT to use force, than neither does the defender. This is NOT the rule in most states anymore.

New Rule:

If the defender has a reasonable belief that force is necessary to protect a third party, then he is justified in using it, even if the third party is not truly in danger. This is the law in most states now.

- The nature of the incident.
- The location (remote, obscure or high-crime area).
- The time of the incident (late night/early morning).
- Objective signs of the adversary's emotional, mental and physical state. You should state how you perceived the subject to be dangerous and how this perception influenced your own mental state (e.g., concerned, fearful, etc.).
- Any and every aggressive action by the subject directed toward you or other third parties. Include verbal threats, gestures, aggressive stances, demeanor, any weapons displayed and applications of force toward the defender.
- Any action by the adversary, such as abrupt movements in an attempt to acquire an object or weapon.
- Any conversation, statements or warnings, if any were made, that you directed to the adversary before the actual physical confrontation. Be sure to describe the adversary's verbal and physical conduct and the reactions (e.g., clenched fists, took a fighting stance, etc.)

You'll also need to describe and identify:

- The assailant, including, but not limited to: sex, race, age, height, weight, build and clothing worn (any unusual bulges that may indicate that the assailant is armed with a weapon). Also include any factors or observations that indicate the subject appeared to be under the influence of alcohol or drugs. An evaluation of strength, physical condition and possible training level and combative skills of the assailant should be articulated. If you had prior contact with the assailant, this information will be relevant to your state of mind.

- Anyone (e.g., friends, relatives of the assailant) who was present, and whether their presence posed an additional potential threat to the safety of you or a third party.
- The force used to overcome the subject's resistance.
- Any techniques and strikes used and the intended target areas and areas actually struck. Should the opponent's actions result in an injury or strike to an unintended area, clearly describe what caused this to occur.
- The force referencing the circumstances that occurred, including any verbal attempts to de-escalate made to the adversary. Articulate any escalation or de-escalation of force and the attenuating reasons (e.g., lack of the effectiveness of the force you used because it had little or no effect on the combatant).
- The combatant's reactions to the force applied.
- Obstacles and difficulties encountered, including fatigue and the inability to overcome injuries received from the adversary.
- The ultimate conclusion of the conflict. Indicate the actions that aided you in overcoming the resistance, eliminating the danger and resolving the conflict.

HANDGUNS

Defenses against Advanced Threats Involving a Handgun

This section deals with extreme, high-risk scenarios in which an assailant, armed with a handgun, poses an imminent threat to the life of the defender under intense conditions. These conditions include threats from all possible angles; threats involving severely stressful and highly dangerous positions; being brutally pushed, punched, kicked, pistol-whipped or moved from point A to point B; being powerfully controlled and restricted by the force of the aggressor and/or the environment; being taken hostage; and being on the ground.

It's true that as variables increase, difficulties analyzing and reacting to the threats also increase. The Krav Maga principles applied to addressing threats and attacks are consistent throughout, and are the reason why Krav Maga works well under extremely stressful conditions. They enable practitioners to assimilate higher-level threats more readily. *Note that the solutions presented in this section assume that no third parties are in danger. Third-party protection is addressed later in the book (see page 95).*

The Weapon

Handguns, which come in many shapes, sizes and types, appear in all scenarios presented here. For this book, there is some value in making a distinction between a semiautomatic handgun and a revolver. While revolvers still outnumber semiautomatics in the U.S., those numbers are narrowing.

It's recommended that if you're training to defend against handgun threats, you should have *at least* a cursory knowledge of the different types of handguns and how handguns work.

Semiautomatic handgun

A semiautomatic has a "slide" on the top of the gun that loads a round (bullet) into the chamber in preparation for the next shot. When held, the slide will not function properly, likely preventing a new round from being loaded

Revolver

and perhaps causing the weapon to malfunction. This is significant if the defender, once making the takeaway, chooses to use the weapon. It will be necessary to "tap and rack," or load another round by clearing the chamber. *Note:* If there is already a round in the chamber, holding the slide will NOT affect that round or prevent it from firing.

A revolver has a cylinder, instead of a slide, that prepares the next round for firing. When held, the cylinder will not turn, preventing a new round from moving into place. This will not cause a malfunction in the revolver. *Note:* If the revolver is already cocked and loaded, holding the cylinder will NOT keep it from firing that round.

Important Note: NEVER train with a live (real) handgun, even if it's unloaded.

The Assailant

Handguns, when carried by criminals, are often used to intimidate, threaten, move, take property or kill. An assailant using a handgun typically derives "power" from the weapon. This is noteworthy, since once an attempted defense is made, the assailant loses this "power" and will also be in a life or death struggle. In the situations presented here, the assailant is within two to four feet (or even less) of the defender, choosing a close proximity to intimidate the defender and disguise his intentions from other parties.

Important Considerations

Critical thinking is essential when attempting to analyze a self-defense situation and determine the best course of action in the moment. When dealing with gun threats, there are many factors that go into establishing the best course of action. In order to do this in "real" time, under stress, you should commit to memory a few tangible (though not concrete) reference points that may serve to reduce reaction time.

In the handgun section, references will be made to "centerline," "live" side, "dead" side, "short" side and "long" side:

Centerline: the relative center of the defender's body

Live side: the side of your body where attacks from the assailant are most readily available (generally thought of as inside the elbows or the front of the body)

Centerline

Movement to live side

Movement to dead side

Short side off to defender's right

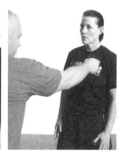

Short side off to defender's left

Dead side: the side of your body where attacks from the assailant are least readily available (generally thought of as outside the elbows or the back of the body)

Short side: this refers to the proximity of the line of fire in relation to the centerline of the defender and the area of the body with the shortest line off the body

Long side: this refers to the proximity of the line of fire in relation to the centerline of the defender and the area of the body with the longest line off the body.

After a disarm is made, the defender has several "after action" options available. Some of these are:

Basic Handgun Defense Principles

Redirect: Move the line of fire off of your body.

Control: Get control of the weapon or weapon hand.

Attack: Send aggressive counterattacks to the assailant.

Takeaway: Disarm the assailant.

- tapping and racking the weapon (make it ready to fire), keeping the assailant in the line of fire
- using the weapon dry or cold (i.e., striking with it)
- using personal weapons/combatives
- accessing own weapon.

Regardless of which action you choose, all should serve to put you in a safer position.

Important Safety in Training Note: Do NOT put your finger on the trigger or at "ready" when training any handgun defenses as it may get broken.

Handgun Threats from the Front

Since Krav Maga is an integrated system, it's common to see techniques learned earlier in the system utilized in more advanced situations at higher levels. Therefore, this section begins with two basic handgun defenses that will serve as the foundation for many of the solutions demonstrated later in the section. In order to simplify assimilation of the information, assume the handgun is being held in the right hand in all of the scenarios given. Generally, the defender's hands are down by the sides. Bringing the hands up and then making a defense is a "bigger" movement that is much more obvious to the assailant. If the assailant orders the defender's hands up, this is an ideal time to make the defense (if in range), since the assailant expects movement.

Basic Gun Threat from Front (Dead-Side Option)

Threat

THREAT The assailant presents the handgun at your centerline or closer to your right. In this case, it is at your chest, although it could be at your head or abdomen.

DANGER You may be shot or taken to another location, where further crimes will be committed.

SOLUTION The line of fire is to your centerline or towards your right, which dictates redirecting the line of fire in that direction.

1 Using the smallest move possible, bring your left hand up and place your index finger at the side of the weapon. Move the weapon in a straight line to your right, bringing your left shoulder forward to increase your reach and blading your body to make you, the target, smaller.

2 Grab the weapon's barrel and turn it sharply away from you, more or less parallel to the ground; begin putting your weight on the weapon as soon as possible.

3 Leading with your left food, immediately burst forward, preferably pinning the gun against the assailant's body (at or near the stomach). Maintaining your weight on the weapon throughout, punch to the assailant's face. *Note:* It may be necessary to throw multiple punches, but you should keep your weight on the weapon and be prepared to continue moving forward in case the assailant is driven back as a result of the strikes.

4 As you recoil your punch, keep your hand and arm close to your body. Reach under the handgun and grab the hammer and sight portion of the weapon. Break the assailant's grip on the weapon by rotating it sharply (about 90°).

5 Pull the weapon back to your body. Do not move your feet until you have complete control of the weapon.

Basic Gun Threat from Front "Cupping" Defense (Live-Side Option)

Threat

THREAT The assailant presents the handgun at your centerline or closer to your left. In this case, it is at your chest, although it could be at your head or abdomen.

DANGER You may be shot or taken to another location, where further crimes will be committed.

SOLUTION The line of fire is to your centerline or towards your left, which dictates redirecting the line of fire in that direction.

1 Using the smallest move possible, bring your right hand up and place your index finger at the side of the weapon. Move the weapon in a straight line to your left, bringing your right shoulder forward to increase your reach and blading your body to make you, the target, smaller.

2–3 Grab the weapon's barrel and turn it sharply away from you, more or less parallel to the ground. Immediately bring your left hand up and under to the hammer portion of the weapon, building a "wall" to maintain control. Maintaining control of the weapon throughout, immediately front kick to the groin.

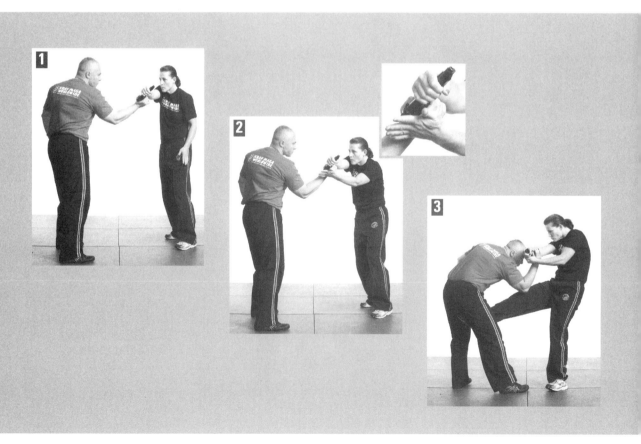

4 Break the assailant's grip on the weapon by turning it sharply towards him and down.

5 Pull the weapon back to your body. Do not move your feet until you have complete control of the weapon.

Note: It is possible to punch then make the cupping technique instead of kicking, but in most cases this is preferred because the control is stronger. It is also possible to redirect to the right and make a cupping technique, but the regular defense (dead-side option; see page 36) is generally preferred.

Gun Threat with Shirt Grab (Centerline)

Threat

THREAT The assailant presents the handgun at your centerline or closer to your right while using his left hand to hold your shirt. He holds the handgun back, close to his body.

DANGER You may be shot or taken to another location, where further crimes will be committed.

SOLUTION You determine that there is enough space between the weapon and the assailant to facilitate a redirection. The line of fire is to your centerline or towards your right, which dictates redirecting the line of fire in that direction. Since the grabbing hand is not causing you to be off balance or pushing you back, this hand is ignored in this defense.

1–5 Blade your body and perform the regular gun from the front defense.

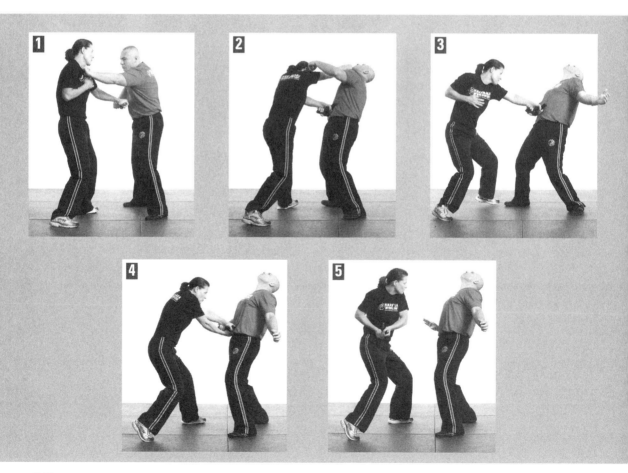

Threat

THREAT The assailant presents the handgun at your centerline or closer to your left while using his left hand to grab your shirt. He is holding the handgun back, close to his body.

DANGER You may be shot or taken to another location, where further crimes will be committed.

SOLUTION You determine there is enough space between the weapon and the assailant to facilitate a redirection. The line of fire is to your centerline or towards your left, which dictates redirecting the line of fire in that direction. Since the grabbing hand is not causing you to be off balance or pushed back, this hand is ignored in this defense.

1–5 In this case, you will defend with the cupping defense.

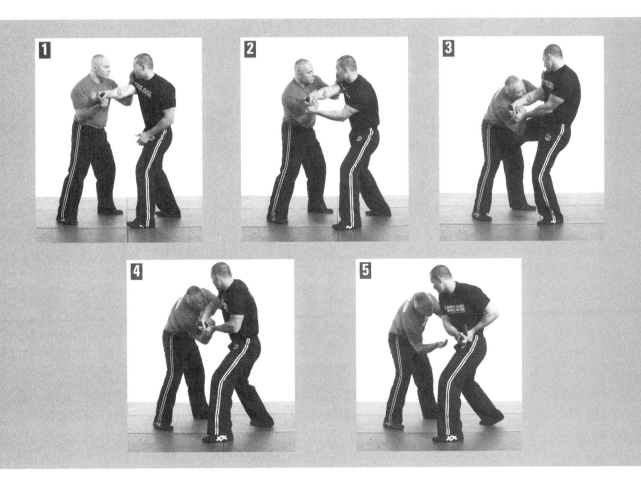

Gun Threat with Hand at Chest (Space for Redirection)

Threat

THREAT The assailant presents the handgun at your centerline or closer to your right and uses his left hand to brace against you or push you backward. He holds the handgun back, close to his body.

DANGER You may be shot or taken to another location, where further crimes will be committed.

SOLUTION You determine that there is enough space between the weapon and the assailant to facilitate a redirection. The line of fire is to your centerline or towards your right, which dictates redirecting the line of fire in that direction. Because your weight is being forced back, the pushing/bracing hand must be addressed.

1 Using the smallest move possible, bring your right hand up to the hand touching you and perform a sweeping motion to clear the assailant's hand (this is similar to an Outside Defense, as shown in *Complete Krav Maga*).

2–5 Blade your body and perform the regular gun from the front defense (dead-side option; see page 36).

Note: It is possible that your hands are up when the threat occurs. In this case, you'll be unable to clear the hand by sweeping from the inside. The solution here is to clear the hand using a plucking motion, similar to the one used in many basic self-defense techniques. The rest of the defense would remain unchanged.

Gun Threat with Hand at Chest (No Space for Redirection)

Threat

This defense is nearly identical to the machine gun takedown presented in *Complete Krav Maga* (page 290).

THREAT The assailant presents the handgun and uses his left hand to brace against you or push you backward. He holds the handgun back, bracing it against his body.

DANGER You may be shot or taken to another location, where further crimes will be committed.

SOLUTION You determine there is not enough space between the weapon and the assailant to facilitate a redirection, and the hand bracing at your chest or even your left shoulder is forcing your weight back.

1 Using your right hand, grab the assailant's left elbow.

2 While lowering your body and pulling yourself forward, pull the assailant's arm towards and past your body using this grip. Stay very close to the assailant, ending up either beside or just behind him. Slide your left arm up and under the weapon arm and pin it to the assailant's body.

3 With the side of your head against the assailant's body, shoot your right hand up and between his legs, as if you're trying to grab his beltline.

4–5 With your hips close to the assailant, lift with your legs (NOT your back) and pull your right arm back towards you. This action should cause the assailant's feet to go up and back and his head to go down towards the ground. *Note:* You do not need to lift the assailant very high off the ground—just a few inches. In actuality, lifting the assailant too high may allow him to spin in towards you.

6 Drive the assailant into the ground, bringing your body down on top of him. As you do this, use elbow strikes to the back of his head. *Note:* The weapon should be under the assailant's body, but it's possible that it was dropped during the takedown and fell away from you. Take note to secure it after rendering the assailant unable to continue fighting.

Gun Threat with Push (Short Side to Left)

Threat

THREAT The assailant presents the handgun at your centerline or closer to your left and uses his left hand to push at the center of your chest. He holds the handgun back, away from his body.

DANGER You may be shot or taken to another location, where further crimes will be committed.

SOLUTION You determine the placement of his hand on your chest makes a right-hand redirection very difficult; also, **your left hand is "inside" of the weapon hand**. The short side is to your centerline or towards your left, which dictates redirecting the line of fire in that direction.

1 Using your left hand, redirect the weapon out and away from the assailant's body.

2 With your right hand, immediately punch to the assailant's face and control the wrist of the weapon hand.

3 To make the takeaway, pull the assailant's wrist towards you and turn the muzzle sharply towards the assailant.

4 Make additional counterattacks.

Reverse angle

Threat

THREAT The assailant presents the handgun at your centerline or closer to your right and uses his left hand to actively push you backward. He holds the handgun back, close to his body.

DANGER You may be shot or taken to another location, where further crimes will be committed.

SOLUTION You determine there is enough space between the weapon and the assailant to facilitate a redirection. The line of fire is to your centerline or towards your right, which dictates redirecting the line of fire in that direction. Because you're being forced back, the pushing hand must be addressed.

1–2 Reaching out, bring your right hand up to the pushing hand and perform a sweeping motion (similar to an outside defense, as shown in *Complete Krav Maga*) to clear this hand. In this case, the motion is also slightly back towards the defender, redirecting the push out and back. Using your left hand, redirect the weapon out and away from the assailant's body. *Note*: The sweeping of the pushing hand requires you to time the push to some degree, so it's important to increase the margin of error by making the motion out away from your body, *not* close to it.

3–6 (Reverse angles shown.) With your right hand, immediately punch to the assailant's face and control the wrist of the weapon hand. To make the takeaway, pull the assailant's wrist towards you and turn the muzzle sharply towards the assailant. Make additional counterattacks.

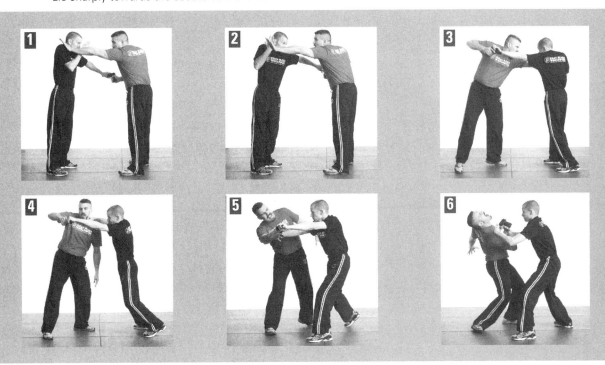

Threat

THREAT The assailant presents the handgun at your centerline or closer to your right and uses his left hand to actively push you backward. He holds the handgun back, close to his body.

DANGER You may be shot or taken to another location, where further crimes will be committed.

SOLUTION You determine there is enough space between the weapon and the assailant to facilitate a redirection, but the assailant has ordered you to put your hands up before approaching. The line of fire is to your centerline or towards your right, which dictates redirecting the line of fire in that direction. Because you're being forced back, the pushing hand must be addressed.

1 Reaching out with your right hand, make a plucking motion to the pushing hand to address the push. In this case, the motion is also slightly back towards you, redirecting the push out and back. Using your left hand, redirect the weapon into the assailant's body. *Note*: The plucking of the pushing hand requires you to time the push to some degree, so it's important to increase the margin of error by making the motion out away from your body, *not* close to it.

2 With your right hand, immediately punch to the assailant's face and continue to perform the regular gun defense from the front technique.

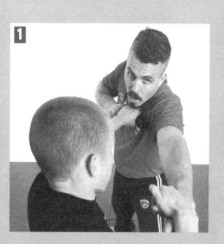

Note: This defense can also be performed when you're caught with your hands down.

Threat

THREAT The assailant presents the handgun under your chin, at your centerline or closer to your right, and uses his left hand to grab your hair.

DANGER You may be shot or taken to another location, where further crimes will be committed.

SOLUTION You determine that the hair grab, as it relates to your ability to make a redirection, causes very little restriction. The line of fire is to your centerline or towards your right, which dictates redirecting the line of fire in that direction. Since the grabbing hand is not restricting your movements, this hand is ignored in this defense.

1–5 Perform the regular gun from the front defense (dead-side option; see page 36). However, since the threat is to the head, a body defense is not necessary. If possible, you should move your head to the left, away from the redirection.

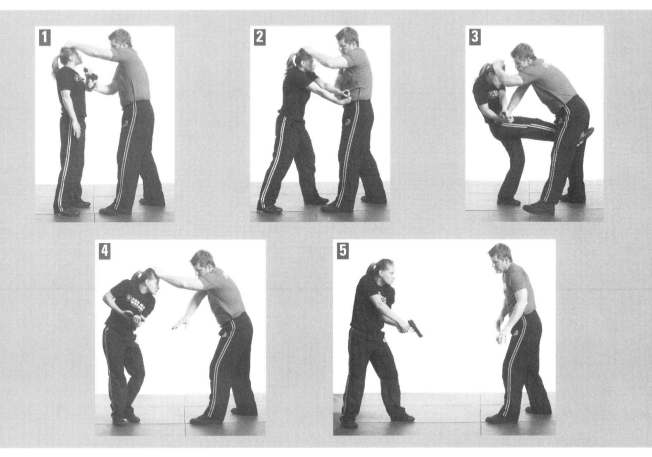

Gun Threat under Chin/Neck, with Hair Grab (Short Side to Left)

Threat

THREAT The assailant presents the handgun under your chin or at your neck and uses his left hand to grab your hair. In this case, the line of fire is to your left side.

DANGER You may be shot or taken to another location, where further crimes will be committed.

SOLUTION You determine that the hair grab, as it relates to your ability to make a redirection, causes very little restriction. The line of fire is to your left, which dictates redirecting the line of fire in that direction. Since the grabbing hand is not restricting your movements, this hand is ignored in this defense.

1–6 Perform the regular cupping defense (live-side option; see page 38). However, since the threat is to the head, a body defense is not necessary. If possible, you should move your head to the right, away from the redirection. Tuck your chin behind your right shoulder.

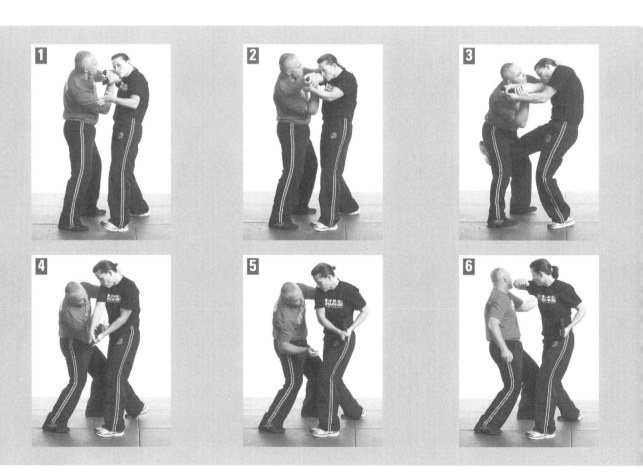

Threat

THREAT The assailant presents the handgun to your side while using his left forearm to pin you against a wall. The short side is to your left as a result of the position the assailant is put in because of the pin.

DANGER You may be shot or taken to another location, where further crimes will be committed.

SOLUTION You determine there is restriction caused by the pin against the wall. The short side is to your left, which dictates redirecting the line of fire in that direction.

1 Redirect the line of fire by grabbing the barrel with your left hand and turning the muzzle to your left.

2–3 Counterattack with a strike to the head with your right hand. To make the takeaway, pull the assailant's wrist towards you and turn the muzzle sharply towards the assailant.

4 Counterattack with further strikes to the head, using the weapon. *Note:* When using a handgun "dry," be sure the line of fire stays away from you at all times.

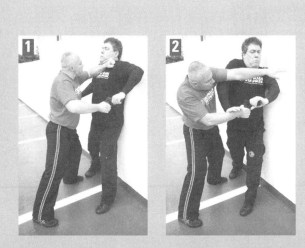

Variation: It's possible that the assailant uses his forearm to apply pressure lower on your chest. In this case, you may choose to redirect the assailant's forearm with your left hand.

Gun Threat over an Obstacle

Threat

THREAT The assailant presents the handgun while you're positioned behind an obstacle such as a table, desk or countertop. While the weapon is presented within reach, the obstacle prevents you from bursting forward and mitigates or eliminates your ability to put weight on the weapon or counterattack.

DANGER You may be shot or taken to another location, where further crimes will be committed.

SOLUTION In this case, the weapon is directed at your centerline. You determine that bursting forward and counterattacking is not feasible or possible, requiring the use of the obstacle to aid in your defense.

1 Perform the cupping technique by redirecting with your right hand and controlling further with your left by cupping at the hammer portion of the weapon.

Variation: If space or position allows, you may pull the weapon hand towards your body and make the takeaway by striking the assailant's wrist down on the edge of the table. It may also be possible, in either scenario, to follow with counterattacks using the weapon and/or punches.

2–5 Break the assailant's grip on the weapon by rotating it sharply (about 90°) and pull the weapon back to your body. Do not move your feet until you have complete control of the weapon.

Threat

THREAT The assailant presents the handgun while you're on your knees.

DANGER You may be shot or taken to another location, where further crimes will be committed.

SOLUTION In this case, the weapon is directed at your centerline. Bursting forward and counterattacking is not feasible or possible because of your body position (it simply takes too long to get up from your knees).

1–2 Perform the cupping technique by redirecting with your right hand and controlling further with your left.

Note: This defense can be made to either direction depending on the environment and the location of the line of fire.

3 Once the "wall" is built, begin rising from your knees, making sure all movements are forward, towards the assailant. *Note:* It is likely the assailant will pull back on the weapon. This action will help bring you up off your knees.

4 Redirecting the line of fire slightly upward, deliver a knee or kick to the groin. A headbutt is also a viable option, but, in this case, the line of fire should not be redirected up.

5–6 Break the assailant's grip on the weapon by rotating it sharply (about 90°) and pull the weapon back to your body. Do not move your feet until you have complete control of the weapon.

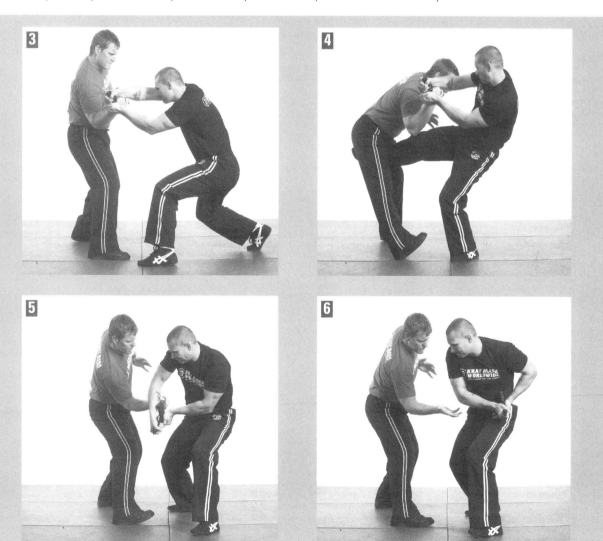

Gun Threat with Defender on Back and Assailant Mounted

Threat

THREAT While you're on your back, the assailant straddles you and holds the handgun to your head.

DANGER You may be shot or taken to another location, where further crimes will be committed.

SOLUTION There are multiple variables in this situation. You must control the weapon and make a takeaway before making a traditional counterattack. In this case, escaping the position is very important.

1 Using your right hand to redirect the weapon to the left, perform the cupping technique. *Note:* The redirection is important—if it's done to the other side, the assailant is likely to use the non-weapon hand to post on the ground and prevent escape.

2 Take the weapon up and away from you, towards the ground, while bucking your hips up. If possible, trap the assailant's foot on the same side with your foot.

3 Buck your hips upward, towards your head and left shoulder, continuing to push the ground with your feet until you end up on top.

4–7 Strike with the weapon, working your way down the assailant's body to the groin, making sure to keep the line of fire away from you.

Note: You should consider your physical state in the "after action" portion of this defense. Since it's likely that a struggle put you there, it may be advisable to maneuver first to your knees then, if you feel ok, up to your feet. Otherwise, operate from your knees until you feel that you can stand without falling back down.

Gun Threat with Defender on Back and Assailant Standing

Threat

THREAT While you're on your back, the assailant stands over you, off to your right side. He leans down a bit, threatening with the handgun.

DANGER You may be shot or taken to another location, where further crimes will be committed.

SOLUTION There are multiple variables in this situation. You must control the weapon while being unable to burst or put weight on the weapon. In this case, your initial response is similar to other, more basic defenses.

1 Using your right hand to redirect the weapon to the left, perform the cupping technique. *Note:* It is also possible to redirect to the right, depending on the shortest line off the defender's body.

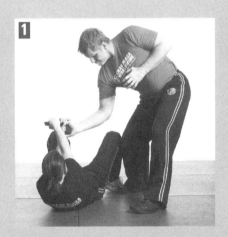

2 Take your right (closest) foot and place it on the assailant's right hip.

3 While kicking off with your right foot, break the assailant's grip on the weapon by rotating it sharply (about 90°) and pull the weapon back to your body.

Handgun Threats from the Back/Side

As previously noted, Krav Maga is an integrated system and, as before, this section will begin with a basic handgun defense that will be the basis for some of the solutions demonstrated later in this section. In order to simplify assimilation of the information, assume the handgun is being held in the right hand in all of the scenarios given.

Important Note: *When threatened from the dead side, it's often hard or impossible to see the weapon without first turning. In all of the defenses described, where possible, it is advised to look and see which hand holds the weapon before deciding a course of action.*

Gun Threat from Behind, Touching (Basic Defense)

Threat

THREAT The assailant presents the handgun, touching the weapon to your lower back. Note that the weapon could be held higher on the back or at the back of the head.

DANGER You may be shot or taken to another location, where further crimes will be committed.

SOLUTION The line of fire is to your centerline or towards your right, which dictates redirecting the line of fire in that direction. Remember, you must look to insure the "off hand" is not actually the weapon hand.

1 Keeping your feet in place and leading with your left arm, turn to face the assailant, redirecting the line of fire by moving the weapon with your arm and blading your body. Reaching your left hand deep under the assailant's arm, burst towards the assailant. Your left foot should be outside of the assailant's right foot.

2–3 Bring your left arm up, trapping the weapon arm against your body. With your right arm, strike with an elbow to the assailant's face while sliding your left arm back to the wrist of the weapon hand. It is important that there are no gaps or spaces between your wrist, the defender's wrist or your body. Your controlling hand should be in a fist and pinned tightly to your body.

4 Counter with knees and/or kicks to the groin (additional upper body combatives are also possible).

5 Bringing your left shoulder slightly forward, reach over with your right hand, pinky side up, and grab the barrel of the weapon. Keep your eyes on the assailant and be sure not to turn your back.

continued on next page

Gun Threat from Behind, Touching (Basic Defense)

continued from previous page

6 To break the grip, snap the muzzle of the weapon down towards the ground, bringing your entire arm down.

7 Lift the weapon straight up for the takeaway.

8 Deliver counterattacks, such as elbows and/or weapon strikes, and get out.

Threat

THREAT The assailant stands with his chest to your back. He loops his left arm around the front of your throat and points the handgun at the side of your head.

DANGER You may be shot or taken to another location, where further crimes will be committed.

SOLUTION Because the assailant is to your dead side and is controlling at least a portion of your body, the redirection and takeaway are made before the counterattack.

1 Bring your hands up towards the handgun, keeping them close to your body and out of sight of the assailant.

2 Using your right hand, grab the barrel and redirect the muzzle forward (this turn should be about 90°).

continued on next page

Gun Threat, Hostage Position

continued from previous page

3–4 Place your left hand at the back of the handgun, building a "wall" of control.

5 Push the handgun forward. Immediately and sharply turn the handgun towards the right. This action will create immense pressure on the assailant's wrist, creating the disarm. While shooting your hips back to further separate the assailant from the weapon, extend both arms forward to completely remove the assailant's hand from the weapon.

6 Turn and counterattack immediately before moving to a safe distance.

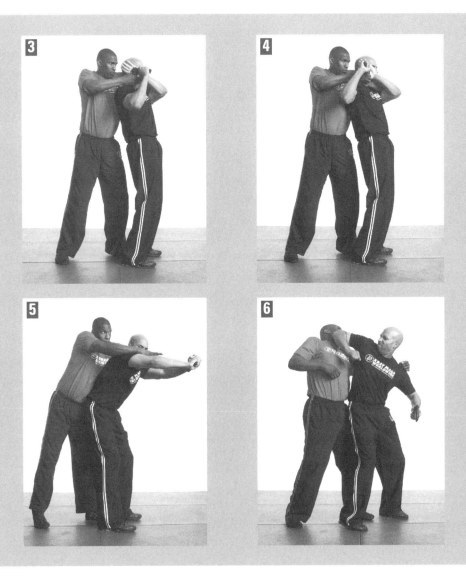

Threat

THREAT The assailant straddles you while you lie face-down on the ground. He holds the handgun at the back of your head.

DANGER You may be shot or taken to another location, where further crimes will be committed.

SOLUTION There are multiple variables in this situation. You must control the weapon and make a takeaway before making a traditional counterattack. In this case, escaping the position is very important.

1 Bring your hands up towards your head, keeping them close to the ground.

2 Using your right hand (assuming your face is turned to the right), grab the barrel and redirect the weapon forward and slightly to the right. The muzzle should be angled away from your face. *Note:* The angle of redirection/placement is important. If the initial round is discharged, any debris should go away from your face, not towards it.

3 With your left hand, control the wrist of the weapon hand while lifting your upper body.

continued on next page

Gun Threat with Defender Face-Down and Assailant Mounted

continued from previous page

4 With your right shoulder at or near the assailant's elbow, drive that shoulder forward and pull the gun back, under your body.

5–6 As the assailant goes over your head, take your body back and under the assailant.

Note: You should consider your physical state in the "after action" portion of this defense. Since it's likely that a struggle put you there, it may be advisable to maneuver first to your knees then, if you feel ok, up to your feet. Otherwise, operate from your knees until you feel that you can stand without falling back down.

Threat

THREAT The assailant is to your left, pressing the handgun at your shoulder while he controls the left side of your body by grabbing your arm with his non-weapon hand. This prevents your ability to turn/spin in.

DANGER You may be shot or taken to another location, where further crimes will be committed.

SOLUTION This situation presents multiple variables but the response should be very familiar to other defenses.

1 Using your right hand to redirect, slide it up your body, concealing it from view as much as possible. Perform the cupping technique. Your left hand will naturally make a "wrist release" when reaching for the control since the thumb of the assailant (the weak part of the grip) will be up.

2 Immediately counterattack with a kick to the groin.

3 Break the assailant's grip on the weapon by turning it sharply towards him and down.

4 Pull the weapon back to your body. Do not move your feet until you have complete control of the weapon.

Threat

THREAT The assailant stands directly behind you, with the weapon held off your body so that there is space between the weapon and the assailant. He places his non-weapon (left) hand on your left shoulder.

DANGER You may be shot or taken to another location, where further crimes will be committed.

SOLUTION Here, the initial redirection is similar to the regular gun from the front defense in that your hand goes straight to the weapon for the redirection.

1 Send your right hand to redirect the weapon (thumb side down) towards the assailant's body. *Note:* Taking your right side shoulder back will serve to blade your body and provide a body defense, but make sure your hand goes first (much like the regular gun from the front defense; see page 36).

2 Leading with your right foot, turn and burst in and immediately punch to the assailant's face with your left hand.

3 Control the wrist of the weapon hand with your left hand.

4–5 To make the takeaway, pull the assailant's wrist towards you and turn the muzzle sharply towards the assailant. Make additional counterattacks.

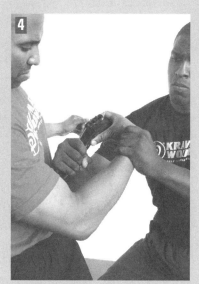

Threat

THREAT The assailant is to your left, pointing the handgun at your side or back. The weapon is at an angle behind your left hand.

DANGER You may be shot or taken to another location, where further crimes will be committed.

SOLUTION Your left hand is "inside" of the weapon hand, dictating that the weapon should be redirected outside or away from the assailant's centerline.

1 Send your left hand to redirect the weapon (thumb side down) out and away from the assailant's body. *Note:* Taking your left shoulder back will serve to blade your body and provide a body defense, but make sure your hand goes first (much like the regular gun from the front defense; see page 36).

2–3 Leading with your left foot, burst in and immediately punch to the assailant's face with your right hand.

4 Control the wrist of the weapon hand with your right hand.

5 To make the takeaway, pull the assailant's wrist towards you and turn the muzzle sharply towards him.

6 Make additional counterattacks.

Gun Threat, Extremely Close Quarters

Threat

THREAT The assailant stands with his chest to your back and holds the handgun to your lower back (centerline or short side left).

DANGER You may be shot or taken to another location, where further crimes will be committed.

SOLUTION You are unable to make the regular defense from behind because the proximity of the assailant's body does not leave room for the regular redirection, forcing you to redirect in the opposite direction. Because of the extreme closeness, the control here is also very different.

1 Keeping your feet in place and leading with your right arm, turn towards your right, redirecting the line of fire by moving the weapon with your arm.

2 Pinning the weapon arm to the assailant's body with your body, grab the assailant's side with your right hand.

3 With your left hand, cover the elbow of the weapon arm to prevent it from being pulled out, further trapping the arm to the assailant's body.

4 If possible, send a knee to the groin.

Reverse angle

5 Move your right hand to the wrist of the weapon hand (avoiding the line of fire) and slide your hand to the gun.

6 Take your left hand from the assailant's elbow to the wrist.

7 To make the takeaway, pull the assailant's wrist towards you and turn the muzzle sharply towards him.

8 Make additional counterattacks.

Note: If the assailant is very close but there is still room to make the regular redirection and defense, do that instead.

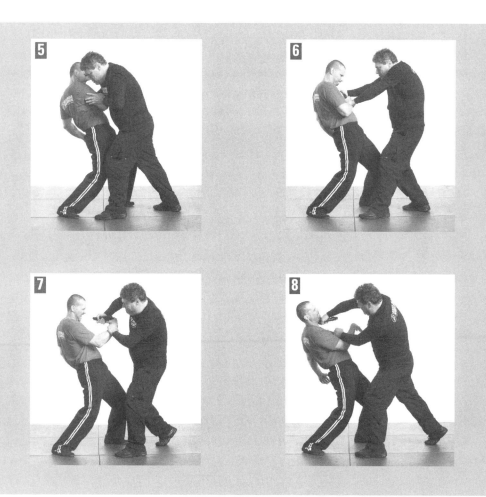

Gun Threat while Being Moved, Handgun Touching

Threat

THREAT The assailant presses the handgun to your lower back and forces you to walk. Note that the handgun could also be held higher on your back or at the back of your head.

DANGER You may be shot or taken to another location, where further crimes will be committed.

SOLUTION You are able to make the regular defense from behind and should do so as soon as possible, since the assailant could stop moving, creating distance.

1–7 Taking as few steps as possible and defending as early as possible, perform the regular gun threat from behind defense (see page 36). *Note:* Footwork is key to this defense. You should make the redirection and turn when the side you're defending to is closest to the assailant. Also, be prepared for the momentum of the assailant to continue, closing the distance quickly as you turn.

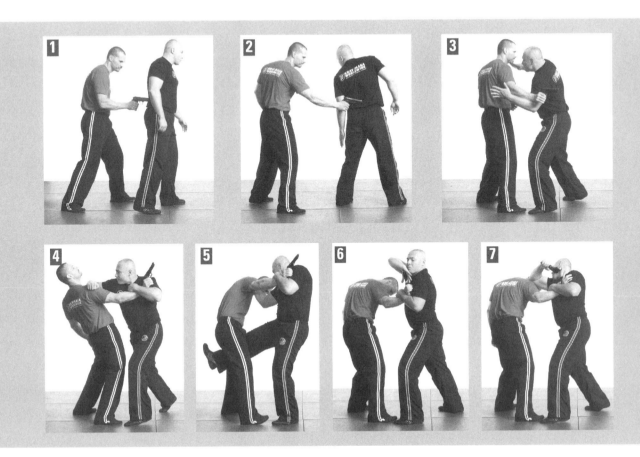

Threat

THREAT The assailant points the handgun at the back of your head while you're on your knees.

DANGER You may be shot or taken to another location, where further crimes will be committed.

SOLUTION Turning and bursting to counterattack is not feasible because of your body position.

1 Bring your hands up towards the handgun, keeping them close to your body and out of sight of the assailant.

2 Using your right hand, grab the barrel and point the muzzle forward, away from you. Place your left hand at the back of the handgun, building a "wall" of control.

3 Immediately and sharply turn the handgun towards the right. This action will create immense pressure on the assailant's wrist, creating the disarm.

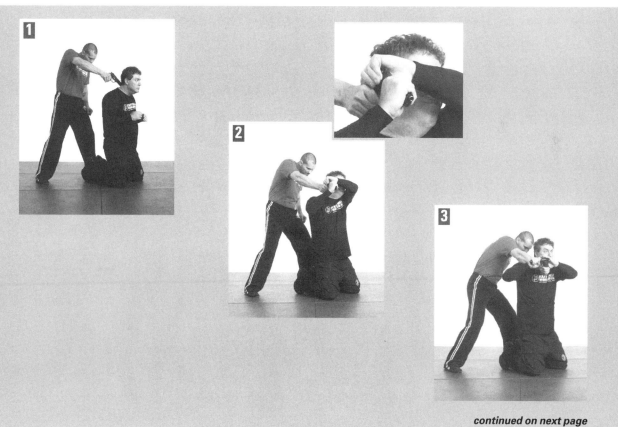

continued on next page

continued from previous page

4 Extend both arms forward to completely remove the assailant's hand from the weapon.

5–7 Turn and counterattack immediately with strikes to the groin before getting up to your feet for further counters and/or disengaging.

> **Variation:** After making the take-away, it may also be possible to shoulder roll forward and away from the assailant before turning to face him.

CARJACKING

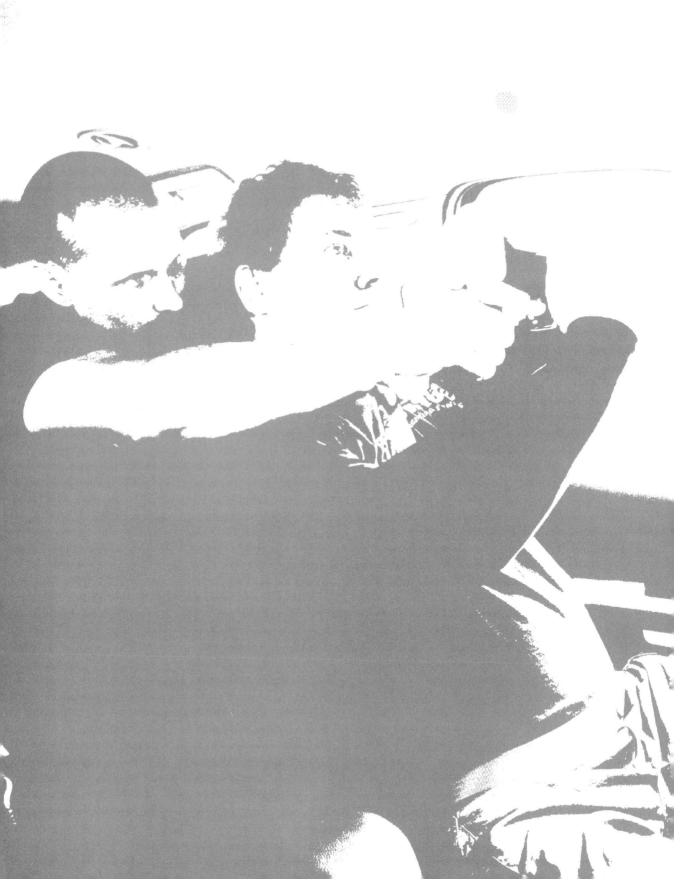

Defenses against Carjacking

Carjacking is defined as the taking of a motor vehicle by the use of force (or threats of use of force) directed at the defender or a third party, with the intent to either temporarily or permanently deprive the driver and/or passenger of the car. The scenarios presented here deal with an assailant with a handgun. Conditions in the environment that affect the defense include, but are not limited to: the car window being up, restrictions placed on the defender by a seatbelt, other passengers in the vehicle, the shape of the seats and/or frame of vehicle, and the distance between the defender and the handgun. Furthermore, the scenarios presented in this section address a driver with no passengers.

The Weapon

Handguns, which come in many shapes, sizes and types, appear in all scenarios presented here. For this book, there is some value in making a distinction between a semiautomatic handgun and a revolver. While revolvers still outnumber semiautomatics in the U.S., those numbers are narrowing. It's recommended that if you're training to defend against handgun threats, you should have *at least* a cursory knowledge of the different types of handguns and how handguns work.

A semiautomatic has a "slide" on the top of the gun that loads a round (bullet) into the chamber in preparation for the next shot. When held, the slide will not function properly, likely preventing a new round from being loaded and perhaps causing the weapon to malfunction. This is significant if the defender, once making the takeaway, chooses to use the weapon. It will be necessary to "tap and rack," or load another round by clearing the chamber. *Note:* If there is already a round in the chamber, holding the slide will NOT affect that round or prevent it from firing.

A revolver has a cylinder, instead of a slide, that prepares the next round for firing. When held, the cylinder will not turn, preventing a new round from moving into place. This will not cause a malfunction in the revolver. *Note:* If the revolver is already cocked and loaded, holding the cylinder will NOT keep it from firing that round.

Important Note: NEVER train with a live (real) handgun, even if it's unloaded.

The Assailant

Handguns, when carried by criminals, are often used to intimidate, threaten, move, take property or kill. In some parts of the country, it's common for assailants to take vehicles in order to commit another crime. In this case, it's possible that the assailant is working with a team that may be nearby and pose a continuing threat even after the initial danger has been eliminated. "After action" tactics will be important to consider, should this be the case.

An assailant using a handgun typically derives "power" from the weapon. This is noteworthy, since once an attempted defense is made, the assailant loses this "power" and will also be in a life or death struggle.

Assailant Outside, Defender in Driver's Seat

In the following scenarios, the assailant approaches the driver's side of the car from one of three angles. The window, in all cases, is down and the assailant presents the weapon just inside, just outside or right at the window/door frame. In order to simplify assimilation of the information, assume the handgun is being held in the right hand in all of the scenarios given. It's worth noting that one viable tactic may be to exit the car then make a defense, if necessary, depending on the demands given by the assailant; however, this is NOT advised if there are passengers, particularly children, in the car.

Approach from Slightly behind Defender

Threat

THREAT This position is the most difficult carjacking situation to deal with because of the position of the assailant in relation to the position of the defender and the limitations presented by the vehicle. The assailant presents the handgun from the rear, exposing little else.

DANGER You may be shot or taken to another location, where further crimes will be committed.

SOLUTION Because of the problems posed by the assailant's angle and the vehicle restrictions, emphasis is placed on redirecting the weapon, gaining control, making a disarm and moving to a more advantageous position. It's important to listen to the demands of the assailant in order to make the movements necessary to execute the best defense. Tactically, it's best to attempt a defense in response to commands to move.

1 Grab the barrel with your right hand and redirect the line of fire, taking your head forward. Pull the handgun slightly inward.

2 Your left hand should immediately come up, pinning the assailant's wrist to the door frame with your wrist. This "control" uses the handcuff principle to keep the weapon hand in place.

continued on next page

Approach from Slightly behind Defender

continued from previous page

3–5 Redirect the muzzle towards the assailant, down against the assailant's thumb, in a quick, explosive movement to make the takeaway.

After-Action Options

It's important to note that you have not delivered any counterattacks to the assailant. Depending on the totality of the circumstances (readiness of vehicle, drive space, seat belt, passengers, third parties, etc.), options may include:

- Tapping and racking the firearm, giving the assailant directions to move away from the vehicle

- Accessing your own firearm, giving the assailant directions to move away from the vehicle

- Driving away

- Leaving the vehicle, finding cover behind the vehicle's engine block, surveying the surroundings

Threat

THREAT The assailant approaches the side of the car door. This position is perhaps the most common since it gives the assailant the best access and concealment from other parties.

DANGER You may be shot or taken to another location, where further crimes will be committed.

SOLUTION Because of the problems posed by the angle and the vehicle restrictions, emphasis is placed on redirecting the weapon, gaining control, making a disarm and moving to a more advantageous position. It's important to listen to the demands of the assailant in order to make the movements necessary to execute the best defense. Tactically, it's best to attempt a defense in response to commands to move.

1 Grab the barrel with your left hand and redirect the line of fire, taking your head backward. *Note:* In order to facilitate the redirection, you may need to reposition your hand. One way of doing this is by moving towards the door handle, as if to open the door.

2 Your right hand should immediately come up, cupping the handgun at the sight and hammer portion. This "control" serves to build a "wall," making it very difficult for the assailant to pull back on the handgun. Tuck your chin.

continued on next page

CARJACKING **83**

Approach from the Side of Defender

continued from previous page

3–4 Pull the handgun in and make the takeaway by slamming the assailant's wrist down on the door frame or steering wheel.

After-Action Options

It's important to note that you have not delivered any counterattacks to the assailant. Depending on the totality of the circumstances (readiness of vehicle, drive space, seat belt, passengers, third parties, etc.), options may include:

- Tapping and racking the firearm, giving the assailant directions to move away from the vehicle

- Accessing your own firearm, giving the assailant directions to move away from the vehicle

- Driving away

- Leaving the vehicle, finding cover behind the vehicle's engine block, surveying the surroundings

Threat

THREAT The assailant approaches the door from the front of the vehicle, most likely presenting the handgun over the side mirror.

DANGER You may be shot or taken to another location, where further crimes will be committed.

SOLUTION Because of the problems posed by the assailant's angle and the vehicle restrictions, emphasis is placed on redirecting the weapon, gaining control, making a disarm and moving to a more advantageous position. It's important to listen to the demands of the assailant in order to make the movements necessary to execute the best defense. Tactically, it's best to attempt a defense in response to commands to move.

1 Grab the barrel with your left hand and redirect the line of fire, taking your head backward and to the left.

2 Your right hand should immediately come up, cupping the handgun at the sight and hammer portion. This "control" serves to build a "wall," making it very difficult for the assailant to pull back on the handgun. Tuck your chin.

continued on next page

Approach from Front of Defender

continued from previous page

3–4 Pull the handgun towards the passenger side, slamming the assailant's face into the windshield or door frame, and make the takeaway by slamming the assailant's wrist down on the door frame or steering wheel.

After-Action Options

It's important to note that you have not delivered any counterattacks to the assailant. Depending on the totality of the circumstances (readiness of vehicle, drive space, seat belt, passengers, third parties, etc.), options may include:

- Tapping and racking the firearm, giving the assailant directions to move away from the vehicle
- Accessing your own firearm, giving the assailant directions to move away from the vehicle
- Driving away
- Leaving the vehicle, finding cover behind the vehicle's engine block, surveying the surroundings

Assailant inside Vehicle

In the following cases, the assailant is inside the vehicle. This poses similar problems, though presented in different ways. As before, your movements will be limited due to space and obstacles, but counterattacks may be easier to make. However, the assailant is also in a position to further attack with personal weapons, which is more difficult when outside of the vehicle.

Assailant in Front Passenger Seat

Threat

THREAT The assailant sits in the front passenger seat and points the handgun at the side of your head.

DANGER You may be shot or taken to another location, where further crimes will be committed.

SOLUTION Because of the problems posed by the angle and the vehicle restrictions, emphasis is placed on redirecting the weapon, gaining control, making a disarm and moving to a more advantageous position. You should note some similarities to the basic response to gun threat to the side of the head (see page 63).

1 Grab the barrel with your right hand and redirect the line of fire, taking your head backward if possible.

2 Your left hand should immediately come up, cupping the handgun at the sight and hammer portion. This "control" serves to build a "wall," making it very difficult for the assailant to pull back on the handgun. Tuck your chin.

continued on next page

Assailant in Front Passenger Seat

continued from previous page

3 Create the disarm by making a quick and explosive movement that forces the muzzle back towards the assailant and down. Use the steering wheel if possible.

4 Counterattack with an elbow to the face and take the handgun back as far from the assailant as possible. *Note:* Additional counters may be difficult if the seatbelt locks into place.

After-Action Options

Depending on the totality of the circumstances (readiness of vehicle, drive space, seat belt, passengers, third parties, etc.), options may include:

- Tapping and racking the firearm, giving the assailant directions to place his arms out the window and look away from you
- Forcing the assailant to exit the vehicle
- Driving away
- Leaving the vehicle, finding cover behind the vehicle's engine block, surveying the surroundings, keeping the assailant in the vehicle

Threat

THREAT The assailant sits in the back seat directly behind you and holds the handgun at your temple/neck area.

DANGER You may be shot or taken to another location, where further crimes will be committed.

SOLUTION Because of the problems posed by the assailant's angle and the vehicle restrictions, emphasis is placed on redirecting the weapon, gaining control, making a disarm and moving to a more advantageous position. You should recognize similarities with this defense to the response to hostage situations outside of a vehicle, with the assailant controlling the hostage from behind (see page 63).

1 Bring your hands up towards the handgun, keeping them close to your body. *Note*: You may be able to use the rear view mirror to better see the assailant, but keep in mind that the assailant may also use the mirror, so your initial movements should be very small and non-aggressive.

2 Using your right hand, grab the barrel and redirect the muzzle towards the front of the vehicle.

3 Place your left hand at the back of the handgun, building a "wall" of control.

continued on next page

Assailant in Rear Seat, Directly behind Driver

continued from previous page

4 Push the handgun forward. *Note:* This action may cause the weapon to discharge into the windshield. There is a chance that fine glass particles may impair your vision. Immediately and sharply turn the handgun towards the right. This action will create immense pressure on the assailant's wrist, creating the disarm.

5 Extend both arms forward to completely remove the assailant's hand from the weapon.

After-Action Options

It's important to note that you have not delivered any counterattacks to the assailant. Depending on the totality of the circumstances (readiness of vehicle, drive space, seat belt, passengers, third parties, etc.), options may include:

- Tapping and racking the firearm and forcing the assailant to exit the vehicle

- Leaving the vehicle, finding cover behind the vehicle's engine block, surveying the surroundings, keeping the assailant in the vehicle

- Following the assailant into the back with counterattacks (but be mindful of the handgun)

THREAT The assailant sits in the back seat behind the passenger side and holds the handgun at your temple/neck area.

DANGER You may be shot or taken to another location, where further crimes will be committed.

SOLUTION Because of the problems posed by the assailant's angle and the vehicle restrictions, emphasis is placed on redirecting the weapon, gaining control, making a disarm and moving to a more advantageous position.

1 Grab the barrel with your right hand and redirect the line of fire, taking your head forward.

2 Control the wrist of the weapon hand with your left hand.

continued on next page

Assailant in Rear Seat behind Passenger Seat

continued from previous page

3–4 To make the takeaway, pull the assailant's wrist towards you and turn the muzzle sharply towards the assailant.

5 Continue to pull the assailant forward in order to make counterattacks.

After-Action Options

It's important to note that you have not delivered any counterattacks to the assailant. Depending on the totality of the circumstances (readiness of vehicle, drive space, seat belt, passengers, third parties, etc.), options may include:

• Tapping and racking the firearm and forcing the assailant to exit the vehicle

• Leaving the vehicle, finding cover behind the vehicle's engine block, surveying the surroundings, keeping the assailant in the vehicle

• Following the assailant into the back with counterattacks (but be mindful of the handgun)

HANDGUNS VS. THIRD PARTIES

Handgun Threats Directed at a Third Party

This section deals with high-risk scenarios in which Krav Maga defensive techniques and principles are designed and used to specifically address an assailant who, armed with a handgun, poses an imminent threat to the life of a third party, such as a family member. While many aspects of these solutions are applicable for use in protective detail for a team charged with defending a subject, this section is not designed for that purpose. Team formations, protocols, goal sets, tools, etc., must be considered and are rarely relevant when a single family member is tasked with defending other family members.

It's true that as variables increase, difficulties analyzing and reacting to the threats also increase. Krav Maga, as an integrated system, is designed with this in mind, allowing practitioners under tremendous duress to perform at a high level of proficiency. The principles that govern addressing threats and attacks are consistent throughout; enabling defenders to assimilate higher level threats more readily.

The Weapon

In all scenarios presented here, the weapon is a handgun. Handguns, which come in many shapes, sizes and types, appear in all scenarios presented here. For this book, there is some value in making a distinction between a semiautomatic handgun and a revolver. While revolvers still outnumber semiautomatics in the U.S., those numbers are narrowing. It's recommended that if you're training to defend against handgun threats, you should have *at least* a cursory knowledge of the different types of handguns and how handguns work.

A semiautomatic has a "slide" on the top of the gun that loads a round (bullet) into the chamber in preparation for the next shot. When held, the slide will not function properly, likely preventing a new round from being loaded and perhaps causing the weapon to malfunction. This is significant if the defender, once making the takeaway, chooses to use the weapon. It will be necessary to "tap and rack," or load another round by clearing

the chamber. *Note:* If there is already a round in the chamber, holding the slide will NOT affect that round or prevent it from firing.

A revolver has a cylinder, instead of a slide, that prepares the next round for firing. When held, the cylinder will not turn, preventing a new round from moving into place. This will not cause a malfunction in the revolver. *Note:* If the revolver is already cocked and loaded, holding the cylinder will NOT keep it from firing that round.

Important Note: NEVER train with a live (real) handgun, even if it's unloaded.

The Assailant

Handguns, when carried by criminals, are often used to intimidate, threaten, move, take property or kill. An assailant using a handgun typically derives "power" from the weapon. This is noteworthy, since once an attempted defense is made, the assailant has lost this "power" and will also be in a life or death struggle. In a scenario involving multiple parties, it's possible that the assailant may be threatening one party to facilitate action from another party.

The Third Party

As indicated, the third party for the purposes of this book is most likely a family member or other loved one (although that is not an absolute, only mentioned to distinguish from a team charged with protection detail). Depending on the nature of the threat, the third party's age, size, physical condition and/or emotional state may be a factor(s) for the defender to consider.

Important Considerations

Please take the time to review the "Important Considerations" detailed on page 34. that are just as relevant here. That said, there are other considerations more specific to third-party protection which should also be examined.

When addressing third-party situations, the first round, as detailed above, becomes even more critical, since your redirection must take into account the line of fire as it relates to you and those around you. That said, when dealing with threats where multiple parties are involved, there is a tactical case to be made for first considering your own safety. The analogy here would be if you were on an airplane in which the cabin lost pressure and the oxygen masks were deployed—you should secure your own mask first. This would insure your ability to then help others. You are NOT to act as cover for a third party; you are there to increase the chances of all surviving the conflict.

Each situation will be different, and your ability to analyze in real time becomes imminently important. Doing scenario training is vital to increasing survivability and decreasing reaction time. You should NOT rely heavily on techniques but on the principles that support the techniques. While this section will show specific and detailed movements, this should simply be a guideline that allows practitioners to extrapolate, using the principles to problem-solve.

Once you've decided to take action, you must be fully committed to the defense. Half-measures will only serve to further exacerbate the situation and will likely result in additional injuries or deaths. Delays will also allow the assailant to recognize your presence, so you should move with decisiveness, speed and aggression. Remember, you're not trying to beat the pull of the trigger but the assailant's recognition of your action and the resulting response. However, your first indication of danger may be as shots are being fired. This does not preclude your defense. Your action may be to stop subsequent rounds from being fired.

Ultimately, your actions should be driven by the basic principles of handgun defense. You should also rely on movements that are fast and make the shortest line to the weapon and off the body.

Important Note: Do not put your finger on the trigger or at "ready" when training any handgun defenses.

Handgun Threats to the Front of the Third Party

Since Krav Maga is an integrated system, it's common to see techniques learned earlier in the system utilized at higher levels, in more advanced situations. The defenses demonstrated here are founded on the basic defenses detailed earlier in this book as well as in Complete Krav Maga.

In order to simplify assimilation of the information, in all of the scenarios given, assume the handgun is being held in the right hand.

Gun to Front of Third Party, Defender behind Assailant

THREAT The assailant points the handgun at the third party's chest, although it could be at the head or abdomen. You are behind the assailant.

DANGER The third party, and others, may be shot or taken to another location, where further crimes will be committed.

SOLUTION You are able to make an approach from behind, defending to the assailant's dead side. You should see similarities in this defense to those found in hand grenade from behind (see page 177) and gun to the side (see page 253 in *Complete Krav Maga*).

1 Moving low so as to remain out of sight, send your hands out as far as possible (palms facing each other), with your left foot landing besides the assailant's right foot.

2 Cover the assailant's wrist with your left hand and the weapon with your right and immediately and explosively redirect the line of fire from the third party.

3 (Reverse angle shown.) Continue the movement by bursting onto your right leg and turning to your left, putting weight on the weapon and turning it towards the assailant and down against his thumb, breaking his grip to facilitate the takeaway.

4 Counterattack immediately, striking with the weapon and moving the assailant away from the third party. *Note:* The line of fire should be towards the assailant at all times, even when striking with the weapon.

Variation: If necessary, you could approach from the opposite angle, making the defense to the live side.

Gun to Front of Third Party, Defender behind Third Party

Threat

THREAT The assailant points the handgun at the third party's chest, although it could be at the head or abdomen. You are behind the third party.

DANGER The third party, and others, may be shot or taken to another location, where further crimes will be committed.

SOLUTION You must approach from behind the third party, defending to the assailant's dead side. The actual defense is almost identical to the regular defense from the front. In this case, the assailant can see you, so furtive moves must be kept to a minimum before acting.

1 Moving quickly, send your right hand to the third party's left shoulder. Your arm should be nearly straight and your hand cupped. Your right foot is next to the third party's left foot. Be sure to send your hand first!

2 Using the third party's body to help launch you forward (enabling you to cover more ground more quickly), pull at the shoulder while bursting forward with your left foot and sending your left hand to the weapon. This action should move you to outside of the assailant's feet, not in front of his body.

3 Redirect the weapon with your left hand while countering with a punch to his face your right hand. At this point, you're making the regular gun from the front defense.

4 As you recoil your punch, keep it close to your body. Reach under the handgun and grab the hammer and sight portion of the weapon.

5 Break the assailant's grip on the weapon by rotating it sharply (about 90°).

6 Pull the weapon back to your body. Do not move your feet until you have complete control of the weapon.

7 If necessary, continue striking, moving the assailant farther away from the third party, being sure to control the weapon and the line of fire.

Note: In a situation where the defender is in close proximity to the gunman, he may be able to reach his right hand to the third party's right (outside) shoulder in order to spin her behind him while making a simultaneous redirection of the line of fire. This action does not propel the defender forward. However, it does place him between the assailant and the third party in a shield-like position.

Handgun Threats from Behind the Third Party

Since Krav Maga is an integrated system, it's common to see techniques learned earlier in the system utilized at higher levels, in more advanced situations. The defenses demonstrated here are founded on the basic defenses detailed earlier in this book as well as in Complete Krav Maga.

Gun to Back of Third Party, Defender to Side (Defense to Dead Side)

Threat

THREAT The assailant ponts the handgun to the third party's lower back, although it could be at the head or upper back. You are standing to the right of the third party.

DANGER The third party, and others, may be shot or taken to another location, where further crimes will be committed.

SOLUTION You must approach from beside the third party, defending to the assailant's dead side. The actual defense is almost identical to the regular defense for gun to the side, in front of the arm, shown in *Complete Krav Maga* (page 257).

Note: If you were more in front of the third party, the regular gun from the front defense may be the best option. This angle makes that defense less practical.

1 Immediately redirect and control the weapon by sending your right hand to the barrel and your left hand to the wrist. Redirect first!

2–3 Continue to turn the weapon, putting weight on it and turning it towards the assailant and down against his thumb, breaking his grip to facilitate the takeaway.

4–5 Counterattack immediately, striking with the weapon and moving the assailant away from the third party. *Note:* The line of fire should be towards the assailant at all times, even when striking with the weapon.

Gun to Back of Third Party, Defender to Side (Defense to Live Side)

Threat

THREAT The assailant points the handgun at the third party's lower back, although it could be at the head or upper back. You are standing to the left of the third party.

DANGER The third party, and others, may be shot or taken to another location, where further crimes will be committed.

SOLUTION You must approach from beside the third party, defending to the assailant's live side. The actual defense is almost identical to the regular defense for gun to the side, in front of the arm, shown in *Complete Krav Maga* (page 257).

1 Immediately redirect and control the weapon by sending your left hand to the barrel and your right hand to the wrist. Redirect first!

2 Continue to turn the weapon, putting weight on it and turning it towards the assailant and down against his thumb, breaking his grip to facilitate the takeaway.

3–4 Counterattack immediately with punches, kicks or knees to the groin and move the assailant away from the third party. *Note:* The line of fire should be towards the assailant at all times, even when striking with the weapon.

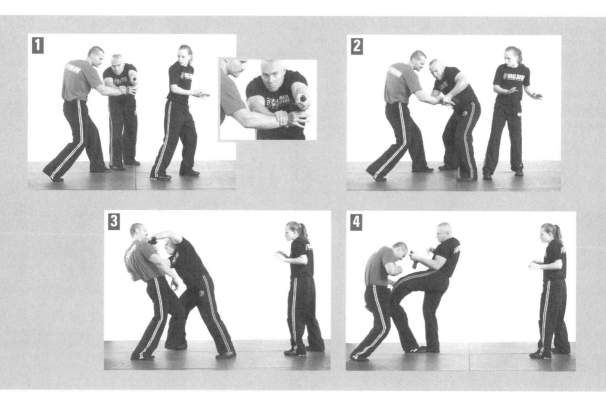

Threat

THREAT The assailant stands with his chest to the third party's back. He loops his left arm around the front of the third party's throat and points the handgun at the side of the third party's head. You are standing to the right of the third party and assailant.

DANGER The third party, and others, may be shot or taken to another location, where further crimes will be committed.

SOLUTION The short side is the center of the third party's head or to the back of the head. The best course of action is to redirect the line of fire towards the assailant. *Note:* Similar actions, with a few minor adjustments, would be taken if you were forced to come from another angle.

1 Grab the barrel with your right hand and redirect the muzzle into the assailant's chest or throat. Control the assailant's wrist with your left hand.

continued on next page

HANDGUNS VS. THIRD PARTIES

Gun to Head of Third Party, Defender to Side (Hostage Situation)

continued from previous page

2 Press the muzzle in and down on the assailant, creating pressure on his chest/throat and separation from the third party, while pulling his wrist back towards you.

3–4 Take the weapon by continuing the downward pressure on the weapon and pulling at his wrist.

5 Counterattack immediately with stomps to his head.

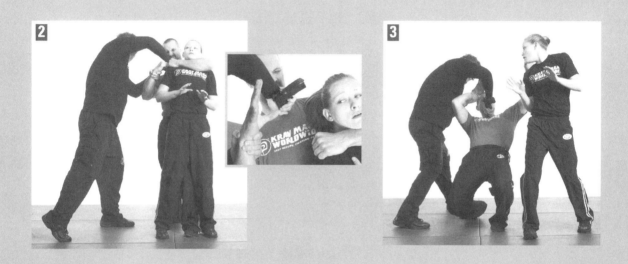

EDGED WEAPONS

Defenses against Threats with an Edged Weapon

This section covers practical and proven techniques to effectively deal with an assailant who uses an edged weapon to pose an imminent threat to the life of the defender. An edged weapon, while typically a knife, could be any short instrument used to cut or stab, such as a broken bottle, scissors, box cutter, screwdriver, etc.

There are several key factors that should be considered when dealing with a threat as opposed to an attack. The behavior of the assailant is different from one who is actively stabbing or slashing at the defender. The assailant may want to gain information or property from the victim, take the victim hostage and/or move the victim to another location. Depending on the nature and context of the threat, a knife-wielding assailant has the ability to threaten the intended victim from close, intermediate and long-range distances, at various angles and heights, and by placing the edged weapon at different parts of the victim's body.

Our experiences have taught us that each passing second may allow the situation to escalate into a more dangerous and dynamic scenario, one where the assailant actively attacks with the edged weapon by stabbing and slashing repeatedly at the intended victim. Just like in basic handgun, the technical principles for addressing knife threats are Redirect, Control, Attack and Takeaway. The tactical responses generally recommended are: (1) escape, (2) use an improvised weapon or shield, and/or (3) engage with personal weapons. This section will address the least desirable but most problematic response—the use of personal weapons. In the cases presented here, the defender has no method of escape or weapons/shields of expedience.

It's also important to note that once an initial defense is made, there are four common responses from the assailant: switch knife hands, thrust the knife forward, pull the knife away, and/or strike. The techniques prescribed here are designed to address all of these concerns. Furthermore, this section will address all of the defensive principles that apply to threats with an edged weapon and will outline defensive techniques and tactics and how to perform them under varying degrees of stress.

Note: Generally, the defender's hands are down by the sides. Bringing the hands up and then making a defense is a "bigger" movement that is much more obvious to the assailant. If the assailant orders the defender's hands up, this is an ideal time to make the defense (if in range), since the assailant expects movement.

The Weapon

An edged weapon may be a dedicated weapon, such as a knife carried on one's person, or a weapon of convenience, such as scissors or broken glass. While the actual attack range is limited, the edged weapon presents multiple problems for defenders.

Edged weapons are easily concealed and, quite often, victims are unaware of the presence of a knife (for example). Edged weapons are typically easy to wield and difficult to isolate for the defender. Such weapons are always "live," never run out of "ammo" and

The Use of Common Objects as Distractions

Common objects used as distractions are often small and, in most cases, easily thrown, such as keys, coins, a wallet, a drink, etc. It's possible that hot liquids or aerosols, when employed as distractions, may also induce pain or injury. Tactically, these objects should be used at the onset of a threat to help facilitate escape or to provide access to a more practical defensive weapon or the use of personal weapons.

When threatened from the front, throw a cup of coffee at the assailant's face and burst in with a kick to the groin.

almost never fail. For these reasons, among others, edged weapons are often considered the hardest to deal with. In addition, according to police reports submitted annually to the FBI, a person in the U.S. who is stabbed by a knife is 20 percent more likely to die than one who suffers a gun shot.

The Assailant

A person willing to use such a weapon is characteristically of a different mindset than those preferring other, longer-range weapons. An assailant choosing to brandish and use an edged weapon is willing to go "hands on"—to get bloody, to feel metal against bone and tendon, and to feel the life leave the victim. A person with this capacity must be met with equal or greater ferocity if the defender is to have a chance of survival.

Basic Knife-Threat Defense Principles

Redirect: Move the edge away from your body.

Control: Get control of the weapon hand.

Attack: Send aggressive counterattacks to the assailant.

Takeaway: Disarm the assailant.

Edged-Weapon Threats from the Front

In order to simplify assimilation of the information, assume the knife is being held in the right hand in all of the scenarios given. The emphasis is almost always on controlling the weapon and counterattacking aggressively. While disarms are shown, the "real" defense is in the offense. Counterattacks should be of a nature that renders the assailant unable or unwilling to continue the attack.

Edged Weapon Touching or at Short Distance off the Body

Threat

THREAT The assailant is close to you and presents the knife to the front of your body.

DANGER The knife may be touching you or simply held close to your body. The knife is not necessarily held statically—the assailant may be moving it around, giving directions, pointing, threatening, etc. The assailant may wish to move you to another location.

SOLUTION Because of the proximity of the threat, you should attempt to control the weapon hand and counterattack aggressively.

1 With your left hand, grab the assailant's weapon-hand wrist, redirecting the weapon towards your right side.

2–3 As soon as possible, reach your right hand to control the weapon hand, covering the hand as much as possible. Extend your arms away from you, applying weight and creating distance. Tuck your chin behind your right shoulder to minimize the chance of being struck in the face.

4 As soon as you attain control, send a front kick to the groin. (If the assailant's body is angled, a round kick to the groin, using the ball of your foot, may be more applicable.) After the initial counterattack, follow with additional counters, maintaining control of the weapon hand and keeping the weapon away from your body. Kicks to the groin and face (if the assailant is doubled over) are preferable.

5 Maintain control at the wrist using your whole body, with the palm of your right hand applying pressure to the knuckles of the assailant's weapon hand. The pressure should force the fingers surrounding the knife to open. While maintaining contact, scrape the weapon out of the assailant's hand.

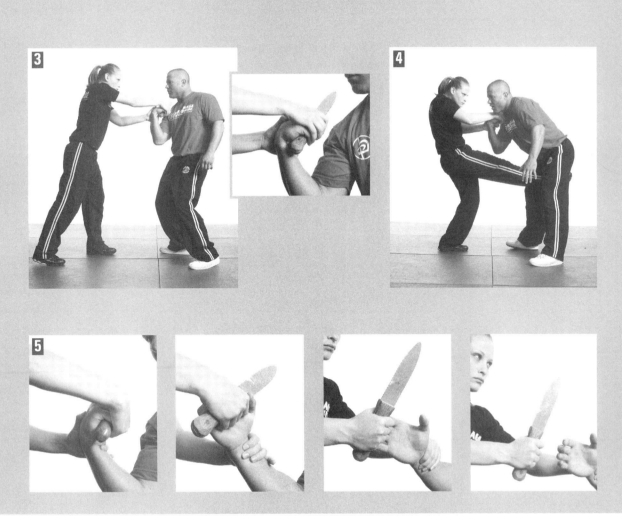

Threat

THREAT The assailant stands further away from you and presents the knife to the front of your body.

DANGER The threat may be the same as with the knife closer to the body but, because of the distance, getting the second hand on quickly is difficult to do. The knife is not necessarily held statically—the assailant may be moving it around, giving directions, pointing, threatening, etc.

SOLUTION Because of the distance, instead of controlling the weapon hand, you should emphasize redirecting the weapon, counterattacking, and escaping or attaining an object that may be used as a weapon or shield.

1–2 Using the palm of your left hand, redirect the weapon hand towards your right with a quick, explosive striking movement to the back of the assailant's hand. *Note:* The redirection is slightly up, which yields less resistance. Your left shoulder should move forward, which angles your body and increases your reach.

3 Immediately after redirecting the weapon hand, advance with a front kick to the groin, moving at an angle in the opposite direction of the redirected weapon hand. Immediately seek to escape or acquire an object that may be used as a shield or weapon.

Threat

THREAT This close-range situation has the weapon likely touching the right side of your neck.

DANGER Here, due to the proximity to the carotid artery, only a small movement by the assailant is required to inflict severe injury or death.

SOLUTION It becomes necessary to recognize the "open" area. In other words, you must analyze the orientation of the weapon as it relates to the direction needed to inflict harm and redirect the weapon in the opposite direction.

1 Using your left hand, grab the weapon hand at the wrist, redirecting it away from your neck, while moving your head in the opposite direction (dead side).

2 Bring your right hand up immediately to cover the weapon hand of the assailant, extending your arms to create space and leverage on the wrist. *Note:* Rotate your redirecting hand so that your palm faces in the direction of the assailant. This action helps facilitate getting the second hand on and offers the palm, as opposed to just the thumb, as a "backstop."

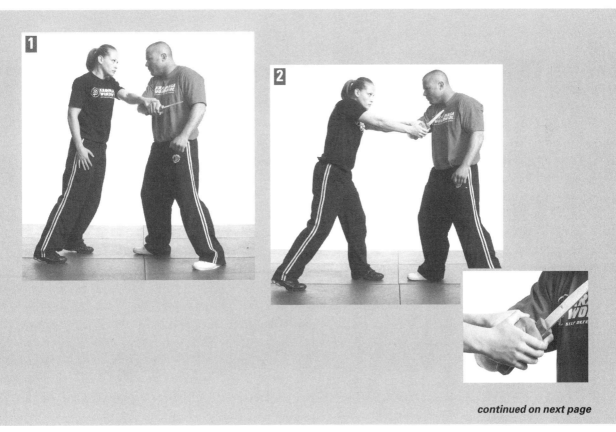

continued on next page

Edged Weapon against Right Side of Neck (Movement to Dead Side)

continued from previous page

3 Immediately after gaining control of the weapon hand, send a front kick to the groin. Send multiple counters, maintaining control of the weapon hand and keeping the weapon away from your body. Kicks to the groin and face (if the assailant is doubled over) are preferable.

4 Maintain control at the wrist using your whole body, with the palm of your right hand applying pressure to the knuckles of the assailant's weapon hand. The pressure should force the fingers surrounding the knife to open. While maintaining contact, scrape the weapon out of the assailant's hand.

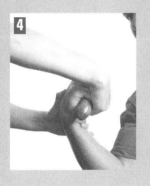

Threat

THREAT This close-range situation has the weapon likely touching the left side of your neck.

DANGER Here, due to the proximity to the carotid artery, only a small movement by the assailant is required to inflict severe injury or death.

SOLUTION It becomes necessary to recognize the "open" area. In other words, you must analyze the orientation of the weapon as it relates to the direction needed to inflict harm and redirect the weapon in the opposite direction.

1 Using your right hand, grab the weapon hand at the wrist, redirecting it away from your neck, while moving your head in the opposite direction (live side).

2 With your left hand, immediately cover the assailant's weapon hand and straighten your arms to create space and pressure. Immediately counterattack with a front kick to the groin.

3 Transition both thumbs to the back of the assailant's weapon hand (at the knuckle line) while maintaining pressure on the wrist (cavalier number 3, as shown in *Complete Krav Maga*, page 265).

continued on next page

Edged Weapon Placed against Left Side of Neck (Movement to Live Side)

continued from previous page

4 Maintaining weight and pressure on the assailant's wrist, move your right hand to cover the assailant's weapon hand and continue to control the assailant's wrist with your left hand (cavalier number 1, as shown in *Complete Krav Maga*, page 263).

5 If necessary or possible, send another kick to the groin, maintaining the wrist control.

6 Using your whole body, maintain control at the wrist, with the palm of your right hand applying pressure to the knuckles of the assailant's weapon hand. The pressure should force the fingers surrounding the knife to open. While maintaining contact, scrape the weapon out of the assailant's hand.

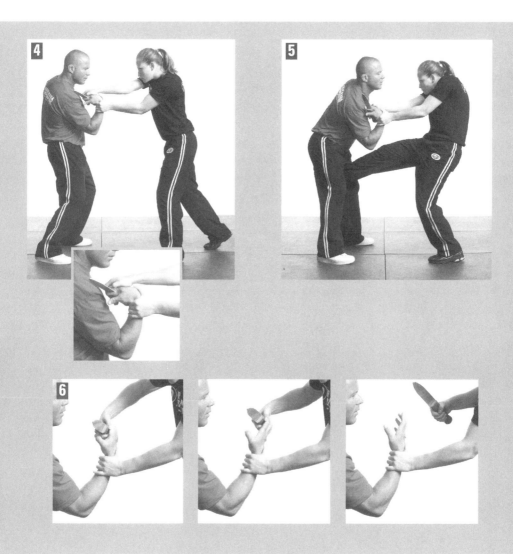

Edged-Weapon Threats from Behind

In order to simplify assimilation of the information, assume the knife is being held in the right hand in all of the scenarios given. The emphasis is almost always on controlling the weapon and counterattacking aggressively. While disarms are shown, the "real" defense is in the offense. Counterattacks should be of a nature that renders the assailant unable or unwilling to continue the attack.

Edged Weapon at Back, Touching

Threat

THREAT The assailant touches the knife to your back.

DANGER While the assailant's intent may be to move you or take property, you are very vulnerable to stabs to the back.

SOLUTION When responding to this threat, it's important to take a quick look over or around your shoulder to determine that the weapon (not the assailant's hand or fingers) is actually at your back and not held in his back hand. Krav Maga practitioners familiar with basic handgun defenses will find the response to this threat very similar.

1 After determining that the weapon is indeed placed at your back, turn towards the left, with your left arm leading the motion.

2 As your left arm redirects the weapon, continue to reach with your left and burst in very deep, reaching your left arm towards the assailant's underarm. Be sure to push the weapon out and away from your body.

continued on next page

Edged Weapon at Back, Touching

continued from previous page

3 Bring your left arm up, trapping the assailant's arm to your body. Your arm should slide to the assailant's wrist while delivering an elbow to the assailant's face with your right arm.

4 Follow the elbow with multiple counterattacks, including knees, kicks, etc.

5 Maintaining control and leverage on the wrist, reach over with your right hand and cover the weapon hand.

6 While applying pressure to the assailant's wrist and shoulder, rotate the weapon hand so that the palm faces up and his fingers are forced open.

7 Without losing contact or control, scrape the knife out of the assailant's hand.

Edged Weapon at Throat from Behind (Hostage Situation)

Threat

THREAT The assailant drapes his weapon arm over your shoulder and places the knife against your throat or neck. Often, you will be pulled backward, compromising balance.

DANGER While the assailant's intent may be to move you or take property, and/or give demands to third parties, you are very vulnerable. With this threat, due to the proximity to the carotid artery and/or throat, only a small movement by the assailant is required to inflict severe injury or death.

SOLUTION Redirect and control the weapon hand while turning to face the assailant and counterattacking. Krav Maga practitioners familiar with basic headlock defenses will find commonality with aspects of this defense.

1 Bring your hands up, keeping them close to your body and concealed from the assailant's sight.

2 Reaching first with your right hand, pluck at the assailant's wrist, redirecting the weapon hand down and away from your neck while immediately adding your left hand for better control. Tuck your chin.

3 Raise your right shoulder to create additional space and leverage.

4 Step out and around the assailant with your left leg. Your head and neck should be tight against the back of the assailant's forearm and triceps area—no space!

5 Transition your left hand to cover the weapon hand and control his wrist with your right hand. Stab with your entire body by advancing toward the assailant.

BLUNT OBJECTS VS. EDGED WEAPONS

Using Blunt Objects against Attacks with an Edged Weapon

This section details realistic and verified techniques using a blunt object to effectively deal with an assailant who is actively attacking with an edged weapon, such as a knife, screwdriver, broken bottle, scissors, box cutter or pen. Blunt objects such as a stick, pipe, tire iron and golf club are typically weapons of convenience, and they often offer the defender the advantage of range and power, depending on the stage of the defender's recognition of the attack. However, it's not feasible to include all angles of attack, positional considerations, blunt-object length, states of recognition, and other variables. The purpose of the section is to introduce readers to the basic techniques, tactics and principles.

There are multiple factors that could be considered when dealing with an edged-weapon attack, but often the defender is unaware of the edged weapon, and the attack may seem like a punch. It is important to note that, for this very reason, Krav Maga Worldwide's curriculum does not distinguish between the two.

The Weapon
An edged weapon may be a dedicated weapon, such as a knife carried on one's person, or a weapon of convenience, such as scissors or broken glass. While the actual attack range is limited, the edged weapon presents multiple problems for defenders.

Edged weapons are easily concealed and, quite often, victims are unaware of the presence of a knife (for example). Edged

The Use of Common Objects as Shields

When using common objects as shields, often the objects available provide coverage due to surface area and/or structural integrity. However, such objects are rarely beneficial as striking implements. In these cases, once the initial defenses are made, as demonstrated in the following section, the shield should be abandoned in favor of personal weapons or escape.

The defender blocks an overhead attack with a gym bag, and then delivers a front kick to the assailant's torso.

The defender uses a trashcan to stop a slash, and then makes an initial counterattack with the trashcan.

weapons are typically easy to wield and difficult for the defender to isolate. Such weapons are always "live," never run out of "ammo" and almost never fail. For these reasons, among others, edged weapons are often considered the hardest to deal with. In addition, according to police reports submitted annually to the FBI, a person in the U.S. who is stabbed by a knife is 20 percent more likely to die than one who suffers a gun shot.

The Assailant

A person willing to use an edged weapon is characteristically of a different mindset than those preferring other, longer-range weapons. An assailant choosing to brandish and use an edged weapon is willing to go "hands on"—to get bloody, to feel metal against bone and tendon, and to feel the life leave the victim. A person with this capacity must be met with equal or greater ferocity if the defender is to have a chance of survival.

The Defensive Weapon

A blunt object, as defined here, is most likely something gleaned from the environment, such as a stick, pipe, tire iron, or golf club. However, the object could also be a gym bag, briefcase, rolled magazine, chair or similar item. Objects like these are chosen to offer the defender the advantage of reach, power and/or surface area when dealing with a knife attack.

When using the blunt object as a weapon (as opposed to a shield), follow-up strikes should be strong and targets should be the head, face, neck and throat regions. The striking surfaces of the blunt object are the tip (4 to 5 inches of the stick farthest from the hand), middle and butt. As a general rule, the tip is preferred since it offers the greatest range advantage and is more powerful.

Edged-Weapon Attacks

In order to simplify assimilation of the information in all the scenarios given, assume the knife is being held in the attacker's right hand and the blunt object in the defender's right hand. While the emphasis of this section is on using blunt objects, do not discount other defenses (such as 360s) or other counters (such as kicks). It's natural to rely heavily on the weapon in hand, but it's important to not be single-minded in your defenses and counters. The defenses and counters used should be those that are most expedient in the moment. Counterattacks should be of a nature that renders the assailant unable or unwilling to continue the attack.

General Response to Any Frontal Attack That Is Recognized Early

ATTACK The assailant shows the knife and his body language suggests a pending attack.

DANGER You may be stabbed or slashed from any angle, on virtually any part of the body, causing serious injury or death.

SOLUTION Because you recognized the attack early on, you should immediately strike to the head and continue to attack aggressively.

1 Strike to the assailant's head and neck region while taking your striking shoulder forward (this action will "blade" your body, making you a smaller target).

2–3 Step away from the edged weapon, continuing to circle the assailant and counterattack. *Note:* The direction of the step depends on your state of recognition. If you recognize the attack very early, the step may be 45° forward and away from the weapon. If the recognition is a bit later, the step may be to the side and away from the weapon.

Attack

ATTACK The assailant stabs straight at you.

DANGER You may be stabbed in the torso, neck or face, causing serious injury or death.

SOLUTION Because of the position of your defensive weapon in relation to the edged weapon, the defense is made to the attacker's live side.

1 As the stab develops, strike the inside of the weapon hand/wrist with the stick, using as much reach as possible, and bringing your left hand up to add more protection.

2 Step away from the weapon hand and strike to the head immediately.

3 Continue striking to the head while circling the attacker.

Note: The direction of the step depends on your state of recognition (this does not refer to the live side/dead side). If you recognize the attack very early, the step may be 45° forward and away from the weapon. If the recognition is a bit later, the step may be to the side and away from the weapon. If the recognition is very late, the step may be 45° back and away from the weapon, but you should still look to advance and circle the assailant if possible.

Attack

ATTACK The assailant stabs straight at you.

DANGER You may be stabbed in the torso, neck or face, causing serious injury or death.

SOLUTION Because of the position of your defensive weapon in relation to the edged weapon, the defense is made to the attacker's dead side.

1 As the stab develops, strike the back of the weapon hand/wrist with the stick, using as much reach as possible, and bringing your left hand up to add more protection.

2 Step away from the weapon hand and strike to the head immediately.

3 Continue striking to the head while circling the attacker.

Note: The direction of the step depends on your state of recognition (this does not refer to the live side/dead side). If you recognize the attack very early, the step may be 45° forward and away from the weapon. If the recognition is a bit later, the step may be to the side and away from the weapon. If the recognition is very late, the step may be 45° back and away from the weapon, but you should still look to advance and circle the assailant if possible.

Ice Pick Stab (Defending to Live Side)

Attack

ATTACK The assailant stabs downward at you.

DANGER You may be stabbed in the torso, neck or face, causing serious injury or death.

SOLUTION Because of the position of your defensive weapon in relation to the edged weapon, the defense is made to the attacker's live side.

1 As the stab develops, strike the inside of the weapon hand/wrist with the tip of the stick, using as much reach as possible, and bringing your left hand up to add more protection.

2 Step away from the weapon hand and strike to the head immediately.

3 Continue striking to the head while circling the attacker.

Note: The direction of the step depends on your state of recognition (this does not refer to the live side/dead side). If you recognize the attack very early, the step may be 45° forward and away from the weapon. If the recognition is a bit later, the step may be to the side and away from the weapon. If the recognition is very late, the step may be 45° back and away from the weapon, but you should still look to advance and circle the assailant if possible.

Attack

ATTACK The assailant stabs downward at you.

DANGER You may be stabbed in the torso, neck or face, causing serious injury or death.

SOLUTION Because of the position of your defensive weapon in relation to the edged weapon, the defense is made to the attacker's dead side.

1 As the stab develops, strike the back of the weapon hand/wrist with the tip of the stick, using as much reach as possible, and bringing your left hand up to add more protection.

2 Step away from the weapon hand and strike to the head immediately. Continue striking to the head while circling the attacker.

Note: The direction of the step depends on your state of recognition (this does not refer to the live side/dead side). If you recognize the attack very early, the step may be 45° forward and away from the weapon. If the recognition is a bit later, the step may be to the side and away from the weapon. If the recognition is very late, the step may be 45° back and away from the weapon, but you should still look to advance and circle the assailant if possible.

Attack

ATTACK The assailant stabs upward at you.

DANGER You may be stabbed in the abdomen, groin or torso, causing serious injury or death.

SOLUTION Because of the position of your defensive weapon in relation to the edged weapon, the defense is made to the attacker's live side.

1 As the stab develops, strike the inside of the weapon hand/wrist with the tip of the stick, using as much reach as possible, and bringing your left hand up to add more protection.

2 Step away from the weapon hand and strike to the head immediately.

3 Continue striking to the head while circling the attacker.

Note: The direction of the step depends on your state of recognition (this does not refer to the live side/dead side). If you recognize the attack very early, the step may be 45° forward and away from the weapon. If the recognition is a bit later, the step may be to the side and away from the weapon. If the recognition is very late, the step may be 45° back and away from the weapon, but you should still look to advance and circle the assailant if possible.

Attack

ATTACK The assailant stabs upward at you.

DANGER You may be stabbed in the abdomen, groin or torso, causing serious injury or death.

SOLUTION Because of the position of your defensive weapon in relation to the edged weapon, the defense is made to the attacker's dead side.

1 As the stab develops, strike the top of the weapon hand/wrist with the tip of the stick, using as much reach as possible, and bringing your left hand up to add more protection. *Note:* This should not be a sweeping motion with the stick but a hard strike.

2 Step away from the weapon hand and strike to the head immediately. Continue striking to the head while circling the attacker.

Note: The direction of the step depends on your state of recognition (this does not refer to the live side/dead side). If you recognize the attack very early, the step may be 45° forward and away from the weapon. If the recognition is a bit later, the step may be to the side and away from the weapon. If the recognition is very late, the step may be 45° back and away from the weapon, but you should still look to advance and circle the assailant if possible.

BLUNT OBJECTS VS. EDGED WEAPONS **137**

Slashing Attack (Defending to Live Side)

Attack

ATTACK The assailant slashes at any angle towards your body and/or head.

DANGER You may be slashed in the torso, neck or face, causing serious injury or death.

SOLUTION Because of the position of your defensive weapon in relation to the edged weapon, the defense is made to the attacker's live side.

1 As the slash develops, strike the inside of the weapon hand/wrist with the tip of the stick, using as much reach as possible, and bringing your left hand up to add more protection.

2 Step away from the weapon hand and strike to the head immediately.

3 Continue striking to the head or other appropriate and vulnerable areas based on the existing level of the threat. It's possible to strike with the butt of the stick so that great force can be generated at a close distance.

Note: The direction of the step depends on your state of recognition (this does not refer to the live side/dead side). If you recognize the attack very early, the step may be 45° forward and away from the weapon. If the recognition is a bit later, the step may be to the side and away from the weapon. If the recognition is very late, the step may be 45° back and away from the weapon, but you should still look to advance and circle the assailant if possible.

ATTACK The assailant slashes at any angle towards your body and/or head.

DANGER You may be slashed in the torso, neck or face, causing serious injury or death.

SOLUTION Because of the position of your defensive weapon in relation to the edged weapon, the defense is made to the attacker's dead side.

Attack

1 As the stab develops, strike the back of the weapon hand/wrist with the tip of the stick, using as much reach as possible, and bringing your left hand up to add more protection.

2 Step away from the weapon hand and strike to the head immediately.

3 Continue striking to the head while circling the attacker.

Note: The direction of the step depends on your state of recognition (this does not refer to the live side/dead side). If you recognize the attack very early, the step may be 45° forward and away from the weapon. If the recognition is a bit later, the step may be to the side and away from the weapon. If the recognition is very late, the step may be 45° back and away from the weapon, but you should still look to advance and circle the assailant if possible.

BLUNT OBJECTS VS. BLUNT OBJECTS

Using Blunt Objects against
Attacks with Blunt Objects

The Krav Maga Worldwide material contained in this section involves obtaining and then using a common object to defend against a variety of impact weapons, such as a hammer, golf club, stick, baseball bat and baton. Here, as in other threat and attack scenarios, the assailant has the ability to attack the intended victim from close, intermediate and long-range distances and at various angles and heights. The attacker can also thrust, stab, swing overhead or diagonally, move horizontally, and more.

For the sake of clarity, the blunt object used by the attacker will be referred to as the "weapon," and the blunt object used by the defender will be referred to as the "defensive weapon." For unarmed defenses against blunt objects, please refer to *Complete Krav Maga.*

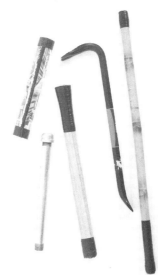

The Weapon
Blunt objects, for the purposes of this section, are likely acquired at the scene of the encounter. Objects such as sticks, pipes, tire irons, golf clubs, hammers and the like are common. These objects, when swung with force, can break bones, cause unconsciousness or even death.

The Assailant
Since blunt objects are often weapons of convenience, it's very possible that the assailant is influenced by adrenaline (rage), fear and/or chemical substances. While this is certainly not an absolute, the possibility of the presence of these variables is surely worth consideration when dealing with such an assailant.

The Use of Common Objects as Shields

When using common objects as shields, often the objects available provide coverage due to surface area and/or structural integrity. However, such objects are rarely beneficial as striking implements because of the lack of hard surfaces or the unwieldy size. In these cases, once the initial defenses are made, as demonstrated in the following section, the shield should be abandoned in favor of personal weapons or escape.

It's worth noting that some objects, such as a fire extinguisher, small briefcase or hairspray can, may be used as a shield and defensive weapon or a distraction and defensive weapon; however, it is important to not rely solely on objects, ignoring your personal weapons.

The defender stops the initial swing of a pipe using a chair, and then kicks the assailant.

The assailant swings at the defender's body with a pipe. The defender uses the fire extinguisher to block the attack and strike to the face.

The Defensive Weapon

Again, blunt objects are most likely gleaned from the surroundings. However, objects used defensively may also include things like gym bags, briefcases, rolled magazines and chairs. These items are useful to shield against attacks but have little to no value for striking.

When using the blunt object as a weapon (as opposed to a shield), follow-up strikes should be strong and targets should be the head, face, neck and throat regions. The striking surfaces of the blunt object are the tip (4 to 5 inches of the stick farthest from the hand), middle and butt. As a general rule, the tip is preferred since it offers the greatest range advantage and is more powerful.

Defenses Using One Hand on the Defensive Weapon

In order to simplify assimilation of the information in all of the scenarios given, assume the weapon is being held in the assailant's right hand and the defensive weapon in the defender's right hand. It's possible to hold the defensive weapon in one or both hands when making the primary defense. This section will detail single-hand defenses before moving on to two-hand defenses, but it's important to note that there are advantages and disadvantages to both, and the decision to use one hand versus two hands should be dictated by the situation.

Defending with one hand on the defensive weapon offers some significant advantages, such as increased range, the ability to redirect and counter faster, and the freedom to check or counter with the non-weapon hand. However, using a single-hand grip tends to require more accuracy and is not as strong as a two-hand grip.

Important note: *While the emphasis of this section is on using blunt objects to defend against blunt objects, do not discount other defenses used in Krav Maga versus blunt-object attacks, or other counters, such as kicks. It's natural to rely heavily on the weapon in hand, but it's important to not be single-minded. The defenses and counters used should be those that are most expedient in the moment. Counterattacks should be of a nature that renders the assailant unable or unwilling to continue the attack.*

Basic One-hand Positions against Outside Attacks

The principles used here should be familiar to basic Krav Maga practitioners. These defenses are, conceptually, very similar to 360° Defenses learned in level 1. Ideally, the hand holding the defensive weapon should be 2 to 4 inches from the butt (end), with the defensive weapon and the arm forming a 90° angle. The defender should attempt to impact the middle of the weapon (or slightly closer to the assailant's hand), not towards the tip of the

Ideal hand position

weapon. Think of punching with the stick, using your body as you would in any other combative.

Note: When using a single-hand grip, the initial block or stop should be perpendicular to the attack. However, for overhead attacks, it's recommended to immediately change the angle to create a deflection in order to clear the weapon and counterattack faster.

Depending on the angle of the attack and the start position of your defending stick, it may be more efficient to defend with the tip of the stick and the thumb of your weapon hand pointing toward the floor.

In addition, the defender's free hand may be used to check or grab the attacking arm to limit continued use of the weapon. This is generally done when the defender has initially and successfully used his stick to stop or redirect the initial attack AND, due to the dynamic, fluid situation, the defender's empty hand is closer to the assailant's attacking arm; the defender's weapon is also further away or out of position to defend or attack.

Attack

ATTACK The assailant swings downward at your head.

DANGER You may be struck in the head, causing serious bodily injury, unconsciousness or death.

SOLUTION Since this attack is overhead, you may use a deflection, as discussed earlier, after the initial block.

1 Send your defensive weapon in the direction of the attack, extending your arm as much as possible and bringing your left hand up to add more protection. Angle your stick so that the assailant's weapon slides down it to minimize the impact on your weapon and your body. Be sure to tuck your head.

2 Step away from the weapon and strike to the head immediately.

3 Continue striking to the head while circling the attacker.

Note: The direction of the step depends on your state of recognition (this does not refer to the live side/dead side). If you recognize the attack very early, the step may be 45° forward and away from the weapon. If the recognition is a bit later, the step may be to the side and away from the weapon.

Three-Quarters Downward Swing

Attack

ATTACK The assailant swings downward at the side of your head, at an angle close to 45°.

DANGER You may be struck in the side of the head or shoulder, causing serious bodily injury, unconsciousness or death.

SOLUTION Because this attack is overhead, you may use a deflection, as discussed earlier, after the initial block.

1 Send your defensive weapon in the direction of the attack, extending your arm as much as possible and bringing your left hand up to add more protection. Be sure to tuck your head.

2 Step away from the weapon and strike to the head immediately.

3 Continue striking to the head while circling the attacker.

Note: The direction of the step depends on your state of recognition (this does not refer to the live side/dead side). If you recognize the attack very early, the step may be 45° forward and away from the weapon. If the recognition is a bit later, the step may be to the side and away from the weapon.

Attack

ATTACK The assailant swings upward at the side of your body, at an angle close to 45°.

DANGER You may be struck in the rib cage, causing serious bodily injury.

SOLUTION

1 Send your defensive weapon in the direction of the attack, extending your arm as much as possible and bringing your left hand up to add more protection. Because of the angle of this attack, you'll need to turn your body to add power and reach to the defense.

2 Step away from the weapon and strike to the head immediately.

3 Continue striking to the head while circling the attacker.

Note: The direction of the step depends on the defender's state of recognition (this does not refer to live side/dead side). If the defender recognizes the attack very early, the step may be 45° forward and away from the weapon. If the recognition is a bit later, the step may be to the side and away from the weapon.

Attack

ATTACK The assailant swings horizontally, like with a baseball bat, to the side of your body.

DANGER You may be struck in the ribcage or arm, causing serious bodily injury.

SOLUTION

1 Send your defensive weapon in the direction of the attack, extending your arm as much as possible and bringing your left hand up to add more protection. Because of the angle of this attack, you'll need to turn your body to add power and reach to the defense.

2 Step away from the weapon and strike to the head immediately. Continue striking to the head while circling the attacker.

Note: The direction of the step depends on your state of recognition (this does not refer to the live side/dead side). If you recognize the attack very early, the step may be 45° forward and away from the weapon. If the recognition is a bit later, the step may be to the side and away from the weapon.

Attack

ATTACK The assailant swings upward to your groin, torso or chin.

DANGER Depending on the position of your body, you may be struck in a number of vulnerable areas, causing serious bodily injury.

SOLUTION

1 Send your defensive weapon in the direction of the attack, extending your arm as much as possible and bringing your left hand up to add more protection. Because of the angle of this attack, you'll need to bend at the waist.

2 Step away from the weapon and strike to the head immediately.

3 Continue striking to the head while circling the attacker.

Note: The direction of the step depends on your state of recognition (this does not refer to the live side/dead side). If you recognize the attack very early, the step may be 45° forward and away from the weapon. If the recognition is a bit later, the step may be to the side and away from the weapon.

Attack

ATTACK The assailant swings in a backhand motion to the side of your head, at a downward angle close to 45°.

DANGER You may be struck in the side of the head or shoulder, causing bodily serious injury, unconsciousness or death.

SOLUTION Because the attack is a backhand swing, your movements and counterattacks will be to the assailant's dead side.

1 Send your defensive weapon in the direction of the attack, extending your arm as much as possible and bringing your left hand up to add more protection. Be sure to tuck your head.

2 Step away from the weapon and strike to the head immediately.

3 Continue striking to the head while circling the attacker.

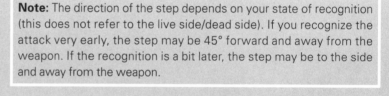

Note: The direction of the step depends on your state of recognition (this does not refer to the live side/dead side). If you recognize the attack very early, the step may be 45° forward and away from the weapon. If the recognition is a bit later, the step may be to the side and away from the weapon.

Attack

ATTACK The assailant swings in a backhand motion to your body or groin, at an upward angle close to 45°.

DANGER You may be struck in the side of the head or shoulder, causing bodily serious injury, unconsciousness or death.

SOLUTION Because the attack is a backhand swing, your movements and counterattacks will be to the assailant's dead side.

1 Send your defensive weapon in the direction of the attack, extending your arm as much as possible and bringing your left hand up to add more protection.

2–3 Step away from the weapon and strike to the head immediately. You may use your free hand to check or grab the attacking arm to limit continued use of the weapon. *Note:* Because of the angle of the defense, gripping the defensive weapon with both hands and striking with the tip of the stick may be the fastest option. Continue striking to the head while circling the attacker.

Note: The direction of the step depends on your state of recognition (this does not refer to the live side/dead side). If you recognize the attack very early, the step may be 45° forward and away from the weapon. If the recognition is a bit later, the step may be to the side and away from the weapon.

Backhand Baseball Swing

Attack

ATTACK The assailant swings horizontally, like with a baseball bat but with a backhand motion, to the side of your body.

DANGER You may be struck in the side of the head or shoulder, causing bodily serious injury, unconsciousness or death.

SOLUTION Because the attack is a backhand swing, your movements and counterattacks will be to the assailant's dead side. Depending on the height of the attack, the defensive weapon may be pointed to the floor or the ceiling. In this case, the attack is a bit lower to the body.

1 Send your defensive weapon in the direction of the attack, extending your arm as much as possible and bringing your left hand up to add more protection.

2–3 Step away from the weapon and strike to the head immediately. You may use your free hand to check or grab the attacking arm to limit continued use of the weapon. *Note:* Because of the angle of the defense, gripping the defensive weapon with both hands and striking with the tip of the stick may be the fastest option. Continue striking to the head while circling the attacker.

Note: The direction of the step depends on your state of recognition (this does not refer to the live side/dead side). If you recognize the attack very early, the step may be 45° forward and away from the weapon. If the recognition is a bit later, the step may be to the side and away from the weapon.

Defenses Using Two Hands on the Defensive Weapon

Defending with both hands on the defensive weapon is a very strong and natural method of defending. It's generally done when the defender has successfully armed himself with an improvised weapon from the zone of danger. This weapon may be heavy, bulky or made of an unwieldy material, such as a wooden chair, a long pole, a fire extinguisher, or a large framed picture. These objects would likely require two hands to be used successfully to defend and counterattack. This two-hand method also offers the defender a great measure of control and accuracy. However, it tends to be a bit slower and the reach is not as great as with a single-hand grip.

Basic Two-hand Positions against Outside Attacks

The principles used here should be familiar to basic Krav Maga practitioners. These defenses are, conceptually, very similar to 360° Defenses learned in level 1. Ideally, the hands holding the defensive weapon should be 1 to 2 inches from the butt (end) and the tip, with the arms extended. The defender should attempt to impact the middle of the weapon (or slightly closer to the assailant's hand) against the middle of the defensive weapon. Think of punching with the stick, using both your hands and your body as you would in any other combative.

Ideal hand position

Since the defenses are designed to cover the body 360° from outside attacks, some of the defenses may overlap. In some cases, the choice of which defense to use depends on the starting position of the defender and the defensive weapon.

Note: When using a two-hand grip, the initial block or stop should be perpendicular to the attack.

Upper Body Swing

Attack

ATTACK The assailant uses a natural swinging motion and targets the area of your body between the side of your head and just above your waistline.

DANGER You may be struck in the side of the head, neck, shoulder or rib cage area, causing serious bodily injury, unconsciousness or death.

SOLUTION This defense covers a very large area of the body, requiring less accuracy and recognition. The hand furthest from the attack "punches" over to meet the attack faster. Movements will be to the attacker's live side.

1 Send your defensive weapon in the direction of the attack, extending your arms as much as possible. Be sure to tuck your head.

2–3 Step away from the weapon and strike to the head immediately. Continue striking to the head while circling the attacker. You may change your grip for counterattacks, if desired.

Note: The direction of the step depends on your state of recognition (this does not refer to the live side/dead side). If you recognize the attack very early, the step may be 45° forward and away from the weapon. If the recognition is a bit later, the step may be to the side and away from the weapon.

Attack

ATTACK The assailant uses a natural swinging motion and targets your head.

DANGER You may be struck on the top of the head or upper shoulder, causing serious bodily injury, unconsciousness or death.

SOLUTION This defense covers a very large area of the head, requiring less accuracy and recognition.

1 Send your defensive weapon in the direction of the attack, extending your arms as much as possible. Be sure to tuck your head.

2–4 Use a sweeping motion to clear the weapon and immediately step in with counterattacks. One option is to kick after making the initial block. Continue striking to the head while circling the attacker. You may change your grip for counterattacks, if desired.

Note: The direction of the step depends on your state of recognition (this does not refer to the live side/dead side). If you recognize the attack very early, the step may be 45° forward and away from the weapon. If the recognition is a bit later, the step may be to the side and away from the weapon.

Lower Body Swing

Attack

ATTACK The assailant uses a natural swinging motion and targets the area between your upper legs and lower rib cage area.

DANGER You may be struck in the knee or lower torso, just at or below the rib cage area, causing serious bodily injury.

SOLUTION This defense covers a very large area of the body, requiring less accuracy and recognition.

1 Send your defensive weapon in the direction of the attack, extending your arms as much as possible. Be sure to tuck your head.

2–3 Step away from the weapon and strike to the head immediately. Continue striking to the head while circling the attacker. You may change your grip for counterattacks, if desired.

Note: The direction of the step depends on your state of recognition (this does not refer to the live side/dead side). If you recognize the attack very early, the step may be 45° forward and away from the weapon. If the recognition is a bit later, the step may be to the side and away from the weapon.

Attack

ATTACK The assailant uses a natural swinging motion and targets your groin, torso or chin.

DANGER Depending on the position of your body, you may be struck in a number of vulnerable areas, causing serious bodily injury.

SOLUTION This defense covers a very large area of the body, requiring less accuracy and recognition.

1 Send your defensive weapon in the direction of the attack, extending your arms as much as possible and bending at the waist, taking the defense forward. Be sure to tuck your head.

2 Use a sweeping motion to clear the we___ ___d immediately step in with counterattacks. One counter option is to strike to the face with the ____ ___fensive weapon after making the initial block.

3–4 Continue striking to the head wh___ ___ay change your grip for counterattacks, if desired.

Note: The direction of the step depends on your state of recognition (this does not refer to the live side/dead side). If you recognize the attack very early, the step may be 45° forward and away from the weapon. If the recognition is a bit later, the step may be to the side and away from the weapon.

Lower Body Backhand Swing

Attack

ATTACK The assailant uses a backhand swinging motion and targets the area between your upper legs and lower rib cage area.

DANGER You may be struck in the knee or lower torso, just at or below the rib cage area, causing serious bodily injury.

SOLUTION This defense covers a very large area of the body, requiring less accuracy and recognition.

1 Send your defensive weapon in the direction of the attack, extending your arms as much as possible. Be sure to tuck your head.

2–3 Step away from the weapon and strike to the head immediately. Continue striking to the head while circling the attacker. You may change your grip for counterattacks, if desired.

Note: The direction of the step depends on your state of recognition (this does not refer to the live side/dead side). If you recognize the attack very early, the step may be 45° forward and away from the weapon. If the recognition is a bit later, the step may be to the side and away from the weapon.

EDGED WEAPON VS. EDGED WEAPON

Using Edged Weapons against Attacks with Edged Weapons

This section details techniques and tactics using an edged weapon (most likely a knife) to efficiently deal with an assailant who is attacking with an edged weapon, such as a knife, screwdriver, broken bottle, scissors, box cutter or pen. There are multiple factors that could be considered when dealing with an edged-weapon attack, but often the defender is unaware of the edged weapon and the attack may seem like a punch. For the purposes of this section, states of readiness will vary, and the defender may be aware of the presence of an edged weapon.

While it's not feasible to include all of the angles of attack, positional considerations, object length, states of recognition, etc., you should take note of the basic techniques, tactics and principles. These aspects generally are consistent and will allow the defender to address an unfamiliar attack. In order to simplify assimilation of the information, in all of the scenarios given, assume the knife is being held in the attacker's right hand and the blunt object in the defender's right hand.

The Weapon

An edged weapon may be a dedicated weapon, such as a knife carried on one's person, or a weapon of convenience, such as scissors or broken glass. While the actual attack range is limited, the edged weapon presents multiple problems for defenders.

Edged weapons are easily concealed and, quite often, victims are unaware of the presence of a knife (for example). Edged weapons are typically easy to wield and difficult for the defender to isolate. Such weapons are always "live," never run out of "ammo" and almost never fail. For these reasons, among others, edged weapons are often considered the hardest to deal with. In addition, according to police reports submitted annually to the FBI, a person in the U.S. who is stabbed by a knife is 20 percent more likely to die than one who suffers a gun shot.

The Assailant

A person willing to use an edged weapon is characteristically of a different mindset than those preferring other, longer-range weapons. An assailant choosing to brandish and use an edged weapon is willing to go "hands on"—to get bloody, to feel metal against bone and tendon, and to feel the life leave the victim. A person with this capacity must be met with equal or greater ferocity if the defender is to have a chance of survival. There are many things about the assailant that are important to recognize in order to implement the best course of action for a successful defense: weight distribution, grip/knife orientation, knife held forward, knife held back, etc. Since the edge/blade is always "live," these factors are often more important in edged-weapon attacks than some other attacks or threats (though not wholly unimportant when dealing with other weapons).

The Defensive Weapon

In this case, the defensive weapon likely has the same attributes as the assailant's weapon. However, the defensive weapon may be familiar to the defender, offering some measure of advantage over a weapon of expedience. It's important for the defender to understand the nature of the defensive weapon: single edge, double edge, point only, etc. It's also generally to the defender's advantage to keep the defensive weapon concealed until making the defense.

Mixing Personal Weapons/Defenses with Defensive Weapon Tactics
It is possible, and advised when prudent, to use your body, in addition to the defensive weapon, to defend and attack.

The defender blocks an overhead attack with a 360 defense while stabbing the assailant's throat.

While the emphasis of this section is on using edged weapons, do not discount other defenses, such as 360s, or other counters, such as kicks. It's natural to rely heavily on the weapon in hand, but it's important to not be single-minded in your defenses and counters. The defenses and counters used should be those that are most expedient in the moment. It's possible to defend with the knife and counter with the knife, defend with the arm and counter with the knife, or defend with the knife and counter with personal weapons. Regardless, counterattacks should be of a nature that renders the assailant unable or unwilling to continue the attack.

Edged-Weapon Defense: Important Points

- Do not show the knife until using it.

- Defend at the assailant's weapon-wielding wrist with the knife.

- Create the strongest defense by forming a 90° angle with your knife and arm.

- Your non-weapon hand should be "active," covering and/or checking the assailant's weapon hand.

- Move as soon as possible, preferably circling to the assailant's dead side.

- If/once dead side is achieved, prevent the assailant from spinning by placing your forearm across his upper back, driving forward and stabbing/slashing.

Attack

ATTACK The assailant shows the knife; his body language indicates a pending attack.

DANGER You may be stabbed in the torso, neck or face, causing serious injury or death.

SOLUTION Because of your early recognition, you should immediately attack the assailant and continue to attack aggressively.

1 Stab to the assailant's throat (or face) while taking your stabbing shoulder forward, lengthening the attack and blading your body. Step forward and at an angle, getting out from in front of the assailant and continuing to circle him and counterattack.

2 Get behind the assailant, controlling him by placing your forearm across his upper back (this control will make it difficult for him to spin).

3 Continue stabbing to his body and slashing at his throat while driving him forward.

Attack

ATTACK The assailant stabs downward to your body or face.

DANGER You may be stabbed in the torso, neck or face, causing serious injury or death.

SOLUTION Because of the position of the defensive weapon in relation to the weapon, the defense is made to the assailant's live side.

1 As the stab develops, strike the inside of the weapon hand/wrist with the blade of the defensive weapon, using as much reach as possible, and bring your left hand up to add more protection or check the weapon hand.

2 Step away from the weapon hand and move forward while slashing to the throat.

3–4 Continue circling the assailant while stabbing and slashing, maneuvering behind him.

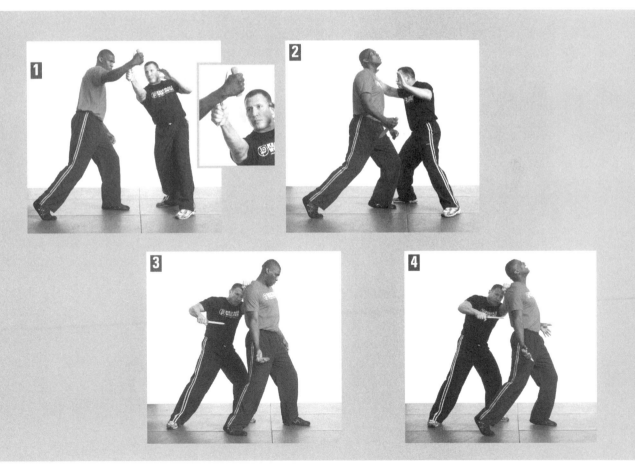

EDGED WEAPON VS. EDGED WEAPON **167**

Attack

ATTACK The assailant stabs straight to your body or face.

DANGER You may be stabbed in the torso, neck or face, causing serious injury or death.

SOLUTION Because of the position of the defensive weapon in relation to the weapon, the defense is made to the assailant's live side.

1 As the stab develops, strike the inside of the weapon hand/wrist with the blade of the defensive weapon, using as much reach as possible, and bring your left hand up to add more protection or check the weapon hand.

2 Step away from the weapon hand and move forward while slashing to the throat.

3–4 Continue circling the assailant while stabbing and slashing, maneuvering behind her.

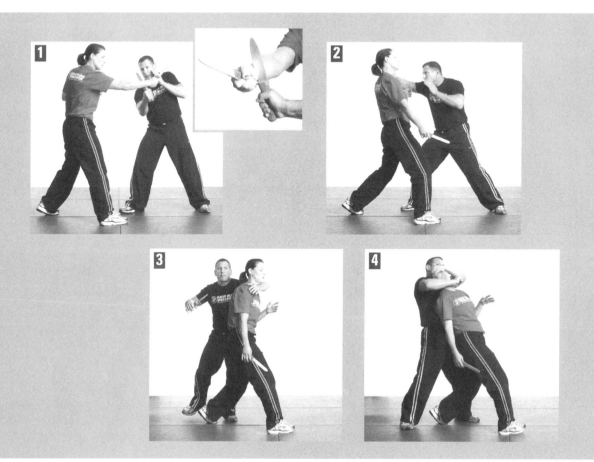

Attack

ATTACK The assailant stabs upward to your body.

DANGER You may be stabbed in the lower torso, causing serious injury or death.

SOLUTION Because of the position of the defensive weapon in relation to the weapon, the defense is made to the assailant's live side.

1 As the stab develops, strike the top of the weapon hand/wrist with the blade of the defensive weapon, using as much reach as possible, and bring your left hand up to add more protection or check the weapon hand.

2 Step away from the weapon hand and move forward while slashing to the throat.

3–4 Continue circling the assailant while stabbing and slashing, maneuvering behind him.

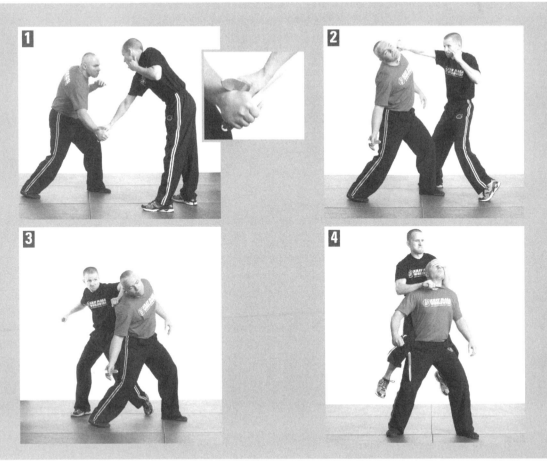

EDGED WEAPON VS. EDGED WEAPON

Attack

ATTACK The assailant slashes at any angle towards your body and/or head.

DANGER You may be slashed in the torso, neck or face, causing serious injury or death.

SOLUTION Because of the position of the defensive weapon in relation to the weapon, the defense is made to the assailant's live side.

1 As the slash develops, strike the inside of the weapon hand/wrist with the blade of the defensive weapon, using as much reach as possible, and bring your left hand up to add more protection or check the weapon hand.

2 Step away from the weapon hand and move forward while slashing to the throat. Continue circling the assailant while stabbing and slashing, maneuvering behind him.

Slashing Attack, Backhand

Attack

ATTACK The assailant slashes at any angle towards your body and/or head.

DANGER You may be slashed in the torso, neck or face, causing serious injury or death.

SOLUTION Because of the position of the defensive weapon in relation to the weapon, the defense is made to the assailant's dead side.

1 As the slash develops, strike the back of the weapon hand/wrist with the blade of the defensive weapon, using as much reach as possible, and bring your left hand up to add more protection or check the weapon hand (at or near the elbow).

2–3 Step away from the weapon hand and move forward while slashing to the throat. Continue circling the assailant while stabbing and slashing, maneuvering behind him.

continued on next page

Off-Angle Variations: It's possible to make defenses to the assailant's dead side if the attack comes from an angle that dictates such a response or if the defensive weapon is very much out of place. Also consider using your free hand to check or grab the attacking arm to limit continued use of the weapon.

Ice pick stab from defender's right: Defender makes the defense with the knife to the outside of the assailant's wrist, slicing downward. Defender immediately bursts in, stabbing to the throat.

HAND
GRENADES

Defending against a Threat by an Assailant with a Hand Grenade

If you tune into the news or conduct a search on the internet, you'll likely find that the use of improvised explosive devices and hand grenades is an increasingly common way to take a hostage, threaten a crowd of people, or inflict mass casualties. What you may be surprised to learn is that encountering this kind of threat (with an explosive device or hand grenade) is not limited to a specific geographical region of the world, such as the Middle East. In fact, on an increasing basis, these threats exist in the United States and other countries. This section addresses how to successfully deal with a threat scenario, usually directed at a third party, where the assailant poses an imminent threat with a hand grenade.

The Weapon

There are many different types of grenades, including fragmentation, concussion, percussion and distraction. While some of these types of grenades were designed to serve different purposes, most are designed to cause serious bodily harm or death, just using different means to accomplish that goal. For the purposes of this book, the focus will be on those grenades designed to kill or maim, particularly fragmentation grenades. In the scenarios presented here, the grenade is used to threaten a crowd or take a hostage.

Fragmentation grenades are normally spherical or cylindrical in design and are typically composed of a body, filler and fuse. The parts of particular concern, when attempting to neutralize such a threat, are the external components: pin and spoon or lever. In order to activate the grenade, the pin most be removed and the lever released, which ignites the fuse, causing detonation. Detonation typically occurs two to five seconds after the release of the lever. *Note:* While it may be possible to retrieve the pin and replace it, finding it is problematic. Furthermore, the action itself requires very fine motor skills and will be difficult under extreme stress.

For the scenarios presented here, it's important to understand the typical "blast zone" of such a grenade. Though it varies, the "kill radius" is generally five meters in all unobstructed directions, with a "casualty radius" of up to fifteen meters.

Note: For the scenarios presented in this book, assume the pin has been removed and you are unable to throw it in a safe direction. If the pin has not been removed or you are able to replace it, further action after the take-away may not be needed.

The Assailant

An assailant willing to use a grenade or similar device is likely prepared to die in the commission of the crime, making such a person much more dangerous than most. Since motivations will certainly vary, this is not always the case, but it is noteworthy. Such a person may be driven by some fervor or passion foreign to some and could be under the influence of alcohol or drugs. These variables will make subduing the assailant incredibly difficult. Should you choose to act, nothing short of total commitment will have a chance of success.

Important Tactical Notes: Keeping the blast radius in mind, the defender, once neutralizing the assailant and taking the grenade, will need to find cover, throw the grenade in an area free of people, or place an obstruction (often the assailant) on top of the grenade and get as far away as possible. If you are forced to run and cover, you should stay as low to the ground as possible. Once reaching the farthest distance in the given time or environment, get down on your stomach, with your feet towards the explosive and your legs crossed. Cover your head with your hands and arms. The idea is to move your head as far away from the explosion as possible and expose as little of your body as necessary.

Threat

THREAT The assailant threatens one or more people with a grenade held in his right hand (this designation is made for the sake of clarity only).

DANGER The grenade could be detonated, causing massive loss of life and/or multiple severe injuries.

SOLUTION You are behind the assailant and must take great care to move swiftly without alerting the assailant of your impending action. This also means minimizing overt movements that may draw the attention of the potential targets, who may inadvertently alert the assailant.

1 Advance towards the assailant, just off the assailant's right shoulder, and send your hands out as far as possible. This will make the defense faster and reduce the recognition time of the assailant. *Note:* Your left foot should be next to the assailant's right foot.

2 Grab the assailant's wrist with your left hand while covering the hand and grenade with your right. The assailant should NOT be able to release the grenade.

3 While turning to face the assailant, continue moving your body until it's completely in front of the weapon hand. Be sure to maintain control of the grenade and weapon hand. *Note:* Your outside foot may leave the ground to increase your reach if the grenade is held high and/or to increase the downward pressure on the wrist.

continued on next page

continued from previous page

4 Burst towards the assailant, applying pressure to the wrist by pulling it towards you and pushing down on the hand, keeping your arms extended.

5 Continue the pressure, pushing the weapon arm outside of the assailant's shoulder and down, taking him back and to the ground. *Note:* This action will cause the assailant to go down and move away from you, so continue moving towards the assailant in order to keep control.

6 Maintaining control of the grenade, hand and wrist, straighten the assailant's arm and immediately begin stomping on his head. *You must completely incapacitate the assailant.*

7 (Reverse angle shown.) Once the assailant is neutralized, scrape out the grenade with your fingers, taking great care to cover and control the lever. *Note:* Maintaining "pain compliance" such as wrist locks or armbars is unnecessary since the assailant should be immobilized as a result of the stomps.

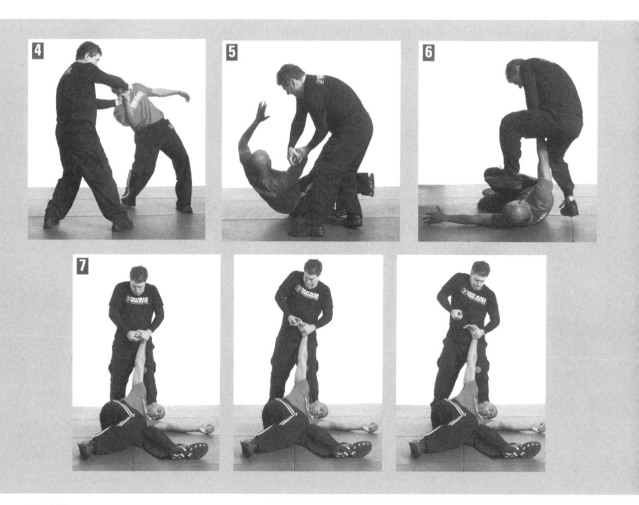

8 Keeping the lever depressed, place the grenade under the assailant's body.

9 Run as far away as the environment and time allow, staying low, quickly moving away from the part of the assailant's body providing the most coverage of the grenade blast.

10 Get down on your stomach, cover your head and cross your legs, with your feet towards the grenade.

Note: While it's possible to take the assailant to the side instead of backward, defending in confined areas such as stores, buses, airplanes or restaurants will limit movement and make lateral takedowns and movements difficult or impossible. Also, if the assailant resists by pulling or pushing, go with the action, maintaining control and performing the takedown. If space allows, do not resist the pull or push.

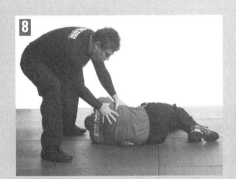

Threat

THREAT The assailant threatens one or more people with a grenade held in his right hand (this designation is made for the sake of clarity only) in a confined area.

DANGER The grenade could be detonated, causing massive loss of life and/or multiple severe injuries.

SOLUTION You are behind the assailant and must take great care to move swiftly without alerting the assailant of your impending action. This also means minimizing overt movements that may draw the attention of the potential targets, who may inadvertently alert the assailant. In this situation, you do not have room to maneuver in front of the assailant.

1 Advance from behind the assailant, just off the assailant's right shoulder, and send your hands out as far as possible. This will make the defense faster and reduce the recognition time of the assailant. *Note:* Your left foot will not be next to the assailant's right since you'll need this space for the takedown.

2 Grab the assailant's wrist with your left hand while covering the hand and grenade with your right. The assailant should NOT be able to release the grenade.

3 While pulling the assailant back and turning towards him, apply pressure to the wrist by pulling it towards you and pushing down on the hand, keeping your arms extended.

4 Continue the pressure, pushing the weapon arm outside of the assailant's shoulder and down, taking him back and to the ground. *Note:* This action will cause the assailant to go down and move away from you, so continue moving towards the assailant in order to keep control.

5 Maintaining control of the grenade, hand and wrist, straighten the assailant's arm and immediately begin stomping on his head. *You must completely incapacitate the assailant.*

6 Once the assailant is neutralized, scrape out the grenade with your fingers, taking great care to cover and control the lever. *Note:* Maintaining "pain compliance" such as wrist locks or armbars is unnecessary since the assailant should be immobilized as a result of the stomps.

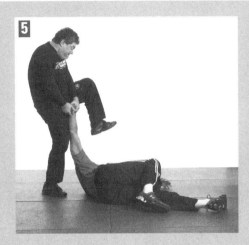

continued on next page

continued from previous page

7 Keeping the lever depressed, place the grenade under the assailant's body.

8 Run as far away as the environment and time allow, staying low, quickly moving away from the part of the assailant's body providing the most coverage of the grenade blast.

9 Get down on your stomach, cover your head and cross your legs, with your feet towards the grenade.

Note: While it's possible to take the assailant to the side instead of backward, defending in confined areas such as stores, buses, airplanes or restaurants will limit movement and make lateral takedowns and movements difficult or impossible. Also, if the assailant resists by pulling or pushing, go with the action, maintaining control and performing the takedown. If space allows, do not resist the pull or push.

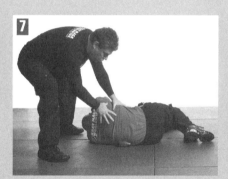

Threat

THREAT The assailant threatens one or more people with a grenade held in his right hand (this designation is made for the sake of clarity only).

DANGER The grenade could be detonated, causing massive loss of life and/or multiple severe injuries.

SOLUTION You are in front of the assailant and may be the target or one of the intended targets. If possible, maneuver close to the assailant without appearing threatening. Once you have committed to a defense, take great care to move swiftly.

1 Advance directly towards the weapon hand and send your hands out as far as possible. This will allow you to get control of the weapon faster.

2 Grab the assailant's wrist with your left hand while covering the hand and grenade with your right. The assailant should NOT be able to release the grenade.

3 Apply pressure to the wrist by pulling it towards you and pushing down on the hand, keeping your arms extended.

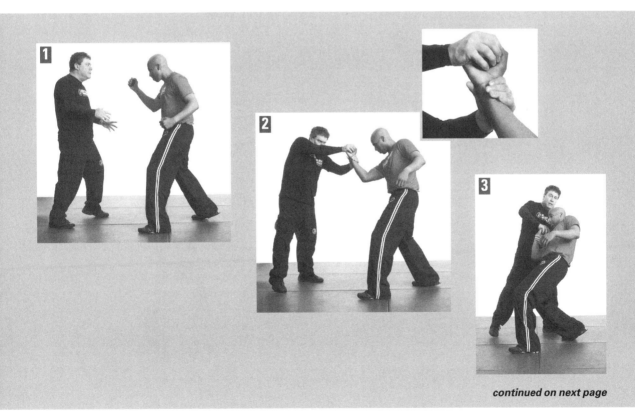

continued on next page

4 Continue the pressure, pushing the weapon arm outside of the assailant's shoulder and down, taking him back and to the ground. *Note:* This action will cause the assailant to go down and move away from you, so continue moving towards the assailant in order to keep control.

5 Maintaining control of the grenade, hand and wrist, straighten the assailant's arm and immediately begin stomping on his head. *You must completely incapacitate the assailant.*

6 Once the assailant is neutralized, scrape out the grenade with your fingers, taking great care to cover and control the lever. *Note:* Maintaining "pain compliance" such as wrist locks or armbars is unnecessary, since the assailant should be immobilized as a result of the stomps.

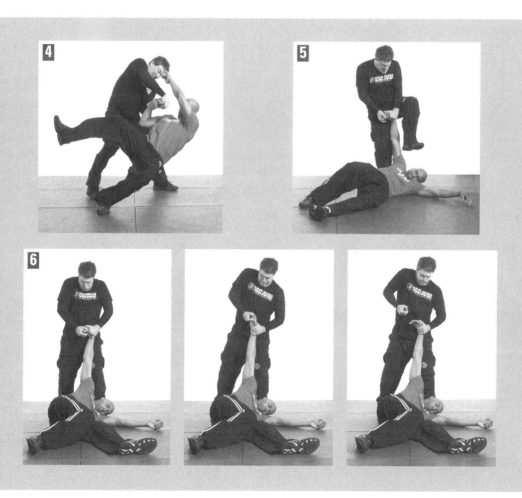

7 Keeping the lever depressed, place the grenade under the assailant's body.

8 Run as far away as the environment and time allow, staying low, quickly moving away from the part of the assailant's body providing the most coverage of the grenade blast.

9 Get down on your stomach, cover your head and cross your legs, with your feet towards the grenade.

Note: While it's possible to take the assailant to the side instead of backward, defending in confined areas such as stores, buses, airplanes or restaurants will limit movement and make lateral takedowns and movements difficult or impossible. Also, if the assailant resists by pulling or pushing, go with the action, maintaining control and performing the takedown. If space allows, do not resist the pull or push.

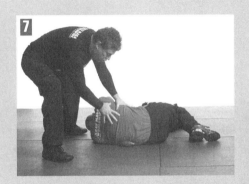

Index

Acknowledgments

It was my honor to be a student and very close friend of Imi Lichtenfeld. He was the most humble man I've ever known. He was thoughtful. He was a clear, concise and gifted thinker. He was an incredible athlete. He was the best teacher I've ever had in any subject, and the person who has most influenced my knowledge and the way I teach the Krav Maga System. Thank you, Imi. And to my other instructors, most notably Lt. Col. Shayke Barak and Sgt. Major Ellie Avikzar, as well as Eyal Yanilov, thank you for teaching Krav Maga with passion and a sense of purpose. And thank you for the valuable lessons you taught me about loyalty and life.

I wish to thank and acknowledge all of the models who participated in the photo shoot for this book, along with the talented staff and instructors of Krav Maga Worldwide. Additionally, certain individuals went above and beyond the call of duty to assist in critical aspects of the creation of Black Belt Krav Maga: Ryan Hoover, Kevin Lewis, Jarrett Arthur, Michael Margolin, Kor Morton, Jon Pascal, Capt. Mitch Tavera, Erin Sheley, S. Daniel Abraham, Joel Bernstein. I offer my sincerest appreciation to them for their time, energy, support and dedication to this project.

* * *

Marni Levine, a 4th degree black belt in Krav Maga, was the highest-ranking female instructor in the world. She was a wife, a wonderful mother, a daughter and sister, and a valiant and true friend. In addition to all that, she was devoted to Krav Maga and worked tirelessly to make it grow. Marni Levine lost her five-year battle with breast cancer at age 37.

As a memorial tribute to an extraordinary woman, Krav Maga Worldwide and STOP CANCER have created The Marni Fund, with a shared mission dedicated to developing improved treatments, new diagnostic procedures and the ultimate goal—a cure for breast cancer. Created in memory of Marni Levine (1969–2006), The Marni Fund is currently supporting innovative breast cancer researchers at UCLA, USC and City of Hope NCI-designated Comprehensive Cancer Centers.

Please help us fight this horrible disease. Donations can be made to The Marni Fund. For more information, please go to www.stopcancer.net/marnifund.php.

Other Ulysses Press Books

Complete Krav Maga: The Ultimate Guide to Over 230 Self-Defense and Combative Techniques

Darren Levine & John Whitman, $21.95

Developed for the Israel military forces, Krav Maga has gained an international reputation as an easy-to-learn yet highly effective art of self-defense. Clearly written and extensively illustrated, *Complete Krav Maga* details every aspect of the system, including hand-to-hand combat moves and weapons defense techniques.

Krav Maga for Beginners: A Step-by-Step Guide to the World's Easiest-to-Learn, Most-Effective Fitness and Fighting Program

Darren Levine, John Whitman & Ryan Hoover, $15.95

Based on simple principles and instinctive movements, Krav Maga is perfect for new students because it is designed to teach real-world self-defense in the shortest time possible. *Krav Maga for Beginners* offers a two-part program of fitness training and street fighting skills that gets the reader in shape and ready to confront an attacker.

Forza: The Samurai Sword Workout: Kick Butt and Get Buff with High-Intensity Sword Fighting Moves

Ilaria Montagnani, $14.95

Transforms sword-fighting techniques into a program that combines the excitement of sword play with a heart-pumping, full-body workout.

Functional Training for Athletes at All Levels: Workouts for Agility, Speed and Power

James C. Radcliffe, $15.95

Teaches all athletes the functional training exercises that will produce the best results in their sport by mimicking the actual movements they utilize in that sport. With these unique programs, athletes can simultaneously improve posture, balance, stability and mobility.